c

# Coordinating assessment practice across the primary school

# THE SUBJECT LEADER'S HANDBOOKS

Series Editor: Mike Harrison, Centre for Primary Education, School of Education, The University of Manchester, Oxford Road, Manchester, M13 9DP

# Coordinating assessment practice across the primary school

Mike Wintle and
Mike Harrison

FALMER PRESS
Taylor & Francis Group

UK    Falmer Press, 11 New Fetter Lane, London EC4P 4EE
USA   Falmer Press, Taylor & Francis Inc., 325 Chestnut
Street, 8th Floor, Philadelphia, PA 19106

First published in 1999

**A catalogue record for this book is available from the
British Library**

ISBN 0 7507 0698 8 paper

**Library of Congress Cataloging-in-Publication Data are
available on request**

Jacket design by Carla Turchini

Typeset in 10/14pt Melior and printed by
Graphicraft Limited, Hong Kong

# Contents

CONTENTS

# List of figures

# Series editor's preface

This book has been prepared for primary teachers charged with the responsibility of acting as coordinators for assessment as well as for those leading various subject areas within their schools. It forms part of a series of new publications that set out to advise such teachers on the complex issues of improving teaching and learning through managing each element and aspect of the primary school curriculum.

Why is there a need for such a series? Most authorities recognise, after all, that the quality of the primary children's work and learning depends upon the skills of their class teacher, not in the structure of management systems, policy documents or the titles and job descriptions of staff. Many today recognise that school improvement equates directly to the improvement of teaching so surely all tasks, other than imparting subject knowledge, are merely a distraction for the committed primary teacher.

Nothing should take teachers away from their most important role, that is, serving the best interests of the class of children in their care and this book, and the others in the series, does not wish to diminish that mission. However, the increasing complexity of the primary curriculum and society's expanding expectations, make it very difficult for the class teacher to keep up to date with every development. Within traditional subject areas there has been an explosion of knowledge and new fields introduced such as science, technology, design, problem solving and health education, not to mention the uses of computers. These are now considered entitlements for primary children. Furthermore, we now expect all children to succeed at these studies, not just the fortunate few. All this has overwhelmed a class teacher system largely unchanged since the inception of primary schools.

Primary class teachers cannot possibly be an expert in every aspect of the curriculum they are required to teach. To whom can they turn for help? It is unrealistic to assume that such support will be available from the headteacher whose responsibilities have grown ever wider since the 1988 Education Reform Act. Constraints, including additional staff costs, and the loss of benefits from the strength and security of the class teacher system, militate against wholesale adoption of specialist or semi-specialist teaching. Help therefore has to come from exploiting the talents of teachers themselves, in a process of mutual support. Hence primary schools have chosen many and varied systems of consultancy or subject coordination which best suit the needs of their children and the current expertise of the staff.

In fact, curriculum leadership functions in primary schools have increasingly been shared with class teachers through the policy of curriculum coordination for the past twenty years, especially to improve the consistency of work in language and mathematics. Since then each school has developed their own system and the series recognises that the one each reader is part of will be a compromise between the ideal and the possible. Campbell and Neill (1994) show that by 1991 nearly nine out of every ten primary class teachers had such responsibility and the average number of subjects each was between 1.5 and 2.2 (depending on the size of school).

These are the people for whom this series sets out to help to do this part of their work. The books each deal with specific issues whilst at the same time providing an overview of general themes in the management of the subject curriculum. The term *subject leader* is used in an inclusive sense and combines the two major roles that such teachers play when they have responsibility for subjects and aspects of the primary curriculum.

The subject focused books each deal with:
- **coordination**: a role which emphasises harmonising, bringing together, making links, establishing routines and common practice; and
- **subject leadership**: a role which emphasises; providing information, offering expertise and direction, guiding the development of the subject, and raising standards.

Other books within the series give guidance on aspects of the curriculum of particular importance to coordinators such special needs, coordination in small schools and preparation for OFSTED re-inspection.

The purpose of the series is to give practical guidance and support to teachers, in particular, what to do and how to do it. They each offer help on the production, development and review of policies and schemes of work; the organisation of resources, and developing strategies for improving the management of the subject curriculum.

Each book in the series contains material that subject managers will welcome and find useful in developing their subject expertise and in tackling problems of enthusing and motivating staff.

Although written primarily for teachers who are assessment coordinators, this book offers practical guidance and many ideas for anyone in the school who has a responsibility for the curriculum including teachers with an overall role in coordinating the whole or key stage curriculum and the deputy head and the headteacher.

In making the book easily readable we have drawn upon our considerable joint experience as primary teachers and headteachers, as an OFSTED lead inspector and as consultants, trainers and advisers to coordinators and others in school faced with issues within assessment, recording and reporting of pupils' progress. The book is not a short cut on 'how to pass' an OFSTED inspection but will give readers a framework to improve teaching and learning through assessment.

We would like to thank the teachers, pupils and governors at Darton Primary School for their help with the production of this book. Mike Wintle is now headteacher at Washingborough Primary School near Lincoln.

Mike Harrison, Series Editor
January 1999

# Chapter 1

# Twelve principles for effective assessment

> ❝ *Assessment is the important ingredient that fuels much of our education system. What right minded teachers have to do is to grasp the assessment nettle and use it to advantage.*
>
> (Clemson and Clemson, 1996)

## The twelve principles of assessment

In a number of schools a policy vacuum (or at the very least a considerable policy confusion) exists with reference to assessment, recording and reporting. According to Campbell's (1993) research team who looked at infant teachers at work

> ❝ *This helps to explain the unduly complex, time consuming and often purposeless assessment and recording activities*
>
> (p. 88)

undertaken by primary teachers. This seminal research recommended that the normal expectations for recording and assessment needed to be clarified, for example the frequency of observation of pupils, the frequency of recording, the numbers of pieces of pupil's work needed for a comprehensive portfolio. They recommended that to do this schools will need to develop their own policies rather than wait for government decree. Soon after this work was published Sir Ron Dearing was appointed to rescue the National Curriculum and assessment in practice but many schools still flounder in their attempt to gain a concerted whole-school approach to the subject.

 *. . . many schools have yet to find an approach to assessment which works effectively and is manageable*          (OFSTED, 1997)

claims Her Majesty's Chief Inspector of Schools.

This book draws on methods which work, and work well, to help to define such policies for, as ever the optimist Paul Black (1998) claims,

 *The subject (assessment) is inescapably central to any educational enterprise. Those who can grasp the concepts that underpin it will be better equipped for all educational work, and might even be able to turn at least some experiences of assessment into enjoyable aspects of learning.*          (p. 6)

The main problem, however, facing any coordinator wanting to help their school to embark upon the sometimes painful process of building and maintaining practice and policy for assessment is where to start! In meeting and working with hundreds of teachers it is obvious that the very thought can turn even the darkest hair grey. Assessment is like that. This subject is so vast that many coordinators simply buy in a ready-made scheme and breathe a sigh of relief. A few months later they often find that things are not quite that simple. The reasons for this are complicated but not altogether surprising. Schools and children, teachers and governors are different and no school is the same as its neighbour. Building a whole-school assessment policy is equivalent to reviewing the whole curriculum; engaging in a complete staff-development programme to review and improve practice; and, getting people to agree and then stick to an agreement which some may not like. As assessment coordinator, if you can appreciate that, reality will start to prevail and you may be able to set realistic time limits to achieve your ends. Even the longest journey starts with the first step.

Based on HMI inspections, OFSTED (1998) have recommended that schools take account of the following features of best practice:

- assessment policies are discussed and implemented by all teachers;
- schemes of work identify the points at which pupils are to be assessed;
- medium-term planning includes clear learning objectives and identifies which aspects of the learning are to be assessed;
- assessment tasks and tests in various subjects are coordinated across the school year;
- records provide a clear indication of pupils' strengths and weaknesses, yet the work involved in maintaining them is kept to a minimum;
- evidence kept to illustrate attainment is discarded once its usefulness is past;
- agreement trialling by the whole team focuses on all the National Curriculum levels represented in the school;
- there is a regular programme for monitoring the implementation of both planning and assessment.

The Task Group on Assessment and Testing (TGAT) under instruction from Margaret Thatcher to produce something

 *which was straightforward, reliable and <u>cheap</u>*    (Galton, 1995)

created a dual purpose regime but was clear in identifying the main purpose of assessment as formative i.e. concerned with recognising children's achievements in order to plan the next steps in their learning. This aspect, however, is not the one which gets the publicity and many teachers almost exclusively identify assessment with allocating children to levels to be used to provide a basis for comparisons between the children themselves, between classes and between schools (Campbell, et al. 1993). Policy pressure, league tables etc. have driven this message home and OFSTED practices have tended to lead readers of their reports to equate quality of teaching with the results achieved. Indeed revised briefing notes for Registered Inspectors (RgIs) indicate that inspectors will be required to place even greater importance on these results than before:

❝ *The purpose of setting out afresh the inspection requirements for attainment and progress is to encourage you (the Registered Inspectors) to:*

- *make more effective use of performance data and its interpretation to report on standards and trends in the school, particularly in the core subjects in primary schools;*
- *focus on weaknesses as well as strengths in the work you see, to be clear about what the school needs to improve;*
- *explain if there are any significant differences between inspection judgments about the standards of work seen and what the performance data says.*

(OFSTED, 1998a, pp. 9–10)

Thus summative purposes are identified with assessment, invoking the fear of children becoming labeled which counters many teachers' value systems. Furthermore, some teachers associate the rise in assessment requirements with league tables and some of the worst educational practices, such as teaching to the test, cramming, the narrowing of the curriculum, and see these infiltrating the primary school at the expense of life-skills, conceptual thought, creativity and collaborative learning. How then can we persuade colleagues to join together to create a set of practices which will fit with their ethical stance against such a background?

Experience has shown that establishing a set of principles and then practising those principles will guide decisions towards an assessment policy and be of real benefit. The principles presented here — twelve in number — have been used by many heads and coordinators as starting points so that the whole staff can look at their existing practice and identify their next course of action. They also provide an ethical backdrop; albeit with a pragmatic approach. We sometimes need guidance and these principles will ensure that we keep our main focus on the children, their learning and improving our own teaching. With such a focus, rather than say, the intention of climbing up a league table, or satisfying yet anther government edict, you might win a few friends.

Putting forward a principled approach could institute a whole
staff introduction to the topic and, through debate of each
issue, give a rapid boost to staff confidence. This method will
lead to the identification of already existing good practice.
You will find, as do the authors, that introducing these ideas
to staff will produce cries of 'we already do that', 'I forgot I
used to do that'. The truth is that no matter how much or how
little attention has been paid to the subject, a great deal of
assessment is already going on but under a different name, for
example marking or observing children in groups and listening
to children read.

Your job is to coordinate these behaviours. Marten Shipman
(1993) writes:

> *Every school has some arrangement for collecting and
> distributing information on the curriculum and the achieve-
> ments of pupils. That information is stored in classrooms,
> departments and headteacher's office. There is rarely any
> discussion of it as a whole. Some of it is duplicated. Some
> of it is collected more than once. Some of it is never used
> once collected . . . that is why the whole staff need to review.
> Some information is jealously guarded as a source of power.*
>
> (p. 67)

The following twelve principles, distilled from the practice
of hundreds of schools, will be useful to you as the basis of
development of an assessment policy (or a means to review the
current one), and will show teachers on your staff that much of
what they do already is valuable, is timely and useful. All they
need is to do it in unison.

**The twelve principles of assessment**
1 The purposes of assessment must be clear, worthwhile and
  agreed by all those involved in the processes.
2 What is to be assessed should be related to the purpose, clearly
  understood and again agreed.
3 Gathering the evidence should become a simple and
  straightforward task.
4 Assessments need to be both systematic and timely.

## Suggestion

Establish a series of meetings with the headteacher to present the current assessment position and the proposed way forward. These meetings need to be well planned and at a time when the head is able to give sufficient uninterrupted time, i.e. not during assembly or first thing in the morning.

Ask if small groups could work on formulating an answer to several questions such as those below and then bring the staff together to seek common ground .

5 The record of the results of assessments must be useful and accessible.
6 Children should be involved in the assessment of their own work and progress.
7 The demands of assessment should enhance good classroom organisation not hinder it.
8 Assessment practices should contribute towards the achievement of equal opportunities.
9 The intended access to children's records should be known before anything is written.
10 Parents and governors should be involved in the creation and monitoring of the assessment policy.
11 The results of assessments of pupils' progress should be reported regularly to parents with appropriate detail.
12 The policy should be reviewed and evaluated regularly.

If you encourage your staff to discuss these twelve principles before attempting to define or redefine your own policy on assessment, or prior to auditing the school's current assessment practice, then you will be able to use it to provide a structured backdrop for these processes to begin. The most effective way in which such principles may be enshrined in the culture of the school is to involve the teachers in setting out such principles and then creating policies and practices which reflect them. One way to do this is to turn the principles into questions. The response to the questions should be sought from key stage groups, year groups, class groups and eventually through bringing the whole staff together. By this time the issues may have been aired a few times and lead to a more productive meeting. You may then go on to work out what the school is doing on each of these fronts at present. There may be some surprises! Use the following structure to achieve this (ask teachers to complete the form before any training day or meeting). For information on the conduct of a training day see Cross and Cross (1993).

| **Assessment policy and practice for the whole school** |
| --- |
| *Gaining agreement on the twelve principles* |

Why should we assess pupils progress?

What should we assess?

How shall we gather evidence about children's learning?

How often do we need to assess pupils?

What is the best way to record what we have found out?

How can we involve children in an assessment of their own progress?

What classroom organisation best supports teacher assessment?

How can assessment practices promote equal opportunities?

Who should have access to records of pupils' progress?

How can parents be involved in the process?

How should we report the results of our assessments?

How shall we evaluate our policy?

## 1: The purposes of assessment

These must be clear, worthwhile and agreed by all those involved in the processes.

It can be argued that assessment is at the very heart of the teaching and learning process. It helps us to: evaluate our own teaching; to consider the strengths and weaknesses of the curriculum; to prioritise our efforts most productively; to diagnose difficulties with individual children and to allow us to pass on information to parents about pupil's progress. Thus assessment interacts with the curriculum, parents, the learners and the teacher.

Thus, despite assessment's poor image among serving teachers, it needs to be recognised that this area is the key to establishing a framework for high quality learning. It is important for staff to meet and agree the main reasons for the initiatives you intend to introduce.

Why do you and your colleagues think you should assess pupils' attainment? Answers to this question which may be given by your colleagues could include any or all of these:

- to find out what the child knows and understands and what he or she can apply;
- to find out how effective our own teaching is;
- to reveal individual children's strengths and weaknesses;
- to inform future teaching; and,
- we have to: it is statutory.

Let us explore each in turn.

Finding out what the child knows and understands and what he/she can apply is something that goes on in everyone's classroom hundreds, perhaps thousands of times every week. Primary teachers haven't traditionally referred to this as an 'assessment' but table tests, spelling checks, and listening to children read all come into this category. Having a whole school policy and recording systematically the results of these day to day judgments, may help teachers to make greater use of activities in which they already, readily engage. Thus we would maximise the return on our efforts.

Research shows that the methods employed by teachers are the key to effective learning, and this is something that the writers hold in common, and hold in common with the majority of the profession. Mortimer et al. (1993), in their research into effective schooling in London, highlighted the importance of heads influencing teaching approach.

> *In schools where all teachers followed guidelines in the same way (whether closely or selectively), the impact on progress was positive. Where there was variation between teachers in their usage of guidelines, this had a negative effect.* (p. 12)

Yet the current debate about the strengths and weaknesses of certain teaching styles, in particular whole-class teaching versus group teaching, is largely uninformed by in-house factual evidence. We often defend our teaching methods as a school, or individually without a shred of evidence that we are right. We also sometimes change our styles and approaches on just such a flimsy basis as well. If assessment is deliberate and the results recorded and compared then the crucial association between the methods we employ and the results we obtain are more likely to emerge. A planned development in assessment needs to have an integral awareness of such issues and this is why it is so important that during the planning stages the methods of teaching are identified at source and an opportunity set up for teacher evaluation (see Chapter 3, Planning).

■ Systematic assessment should reveal children's individual strengths and weaknesses and help to identify and diagnose problems. There are three ways in which teachers can assess children's work: observation, perusal of children's work; and by questioning or discussion. The best examples allow the teacher to pick up on what additional teaching is needed, came about through marking and levelling classwork.

■ Increasing teachers' ability to select future teaching content is the most important reason why assessment should be at the forefront of any curriculum initiative and makes a convincing argument when the assessment coordinator is confronted by overworked staff or a reluctant headteacher. By carefully assessing the achievements of the pupils in his/her class the teacher should have a good idea

**Suggestion**

Establish with the headteacher a framework for improving assessment practice within the school. This means that you, as assessment coordinator, will need to negotiate staff development time, and time for staff meetings, briefings and a place in the school development plan.

about the progress his/her charges have made and where to go next. It is, if you like, the very map that identifies for the teacher the journey described in the later chapter on planning.

It needs to be remembered that one of the reasons that teachers assess children's achievements is because they have to! The following guidelines are based on the 1988 Education Act.

**Schools are required to:**
- Teach the National Curriculum and RE
- Administer Standard Assessment Tests
- Maintain records on pupil attainment in the National Curriculum
- Make Teacher Assessments in the three core subjects to provide levels at the end of each key stage
- Report on pupils' progress to parents (at least once a year)
- Provide assessment data to the LEA or other nominated body

The reasons for national measures are embedded in the reasons for the National Curriculum, namely to raise standards and to improve performance in scientific and technological areas.

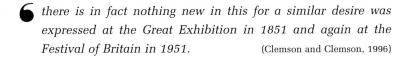

*there is in fact nothing new in this for a similar desire was expressed at the Great Exhibition in 1851 and again at the Festival of Britain in 1951.* (Clemson and Clemson, 1996)

We shall probably see a repeat of this once more in our lifetimes. In order to raise standards, the desired standards have to be clearly stated (the National Curriculum) and current standards identified (statutory assessment requirements).

## 2: What is to be assessed

What is to be assessed should be related to the purpose, clearly understood and agreed.

It is not necessary to assess everything currently undertaken by the child in the classroom and

| What should we assess? |

❛ *Nor should we try . . . Records should be useful, manageable and easy to interpret* (Sir Ron Dearing, DFE, 1994)

■ To keep the process manageable we need to prioritise the significant aspects within the core subjects. To meet with current national priorities we should concentrate particularly on English Attainment Targets 2 and 3 (reading and writing), maths Attainment Targets 2, 3 and 4 (number, measures and data handling) and science Attainment Target 1.
■ What we assess should be left to the professional responsibility of the teacher.
■ Aspects which contribute to Standard Assessments (SATs) at the end of each key stage should be looked at carefully.

The problem many teachers have with assessment is the acceptance by those who do not have to do it that it is possible and practical to assess everything that goes on inside (and indeed outside) the classroom. This misunderstanding was the overriding reason why assessment became removed from teaching reality and devoid of much practical development. Vic Kelly wrote in 1992 that

❛ *Assessment can determine not only the content of our curriculum it can also determine the nature of our curriculum. Indeed the very concept of curriculum which we adopt and base our work as teachers upon.* (Kelly, 1992, p. 17)

And here lies the practical danger of assessment. With a 'let's assess everything' approach the work overload would mean that assessment dominated the curriculum and that classroom learning would be smothered. Multiplied across a number of schools, the net result where this happened frequently led to poor assessment strategies, and wasted time and effort. A secondary feature even when schools were successful, meant that teachers became disillusioned about anything to do with assessment. Development of practice in this aspect is many years behind most other curricular developments.

Senior educationalists have not been unaware of the problems. A DES (1991) report found that infant teachers have, on average, only 22 minutes of non-contact time per week (compared to an average of 3 hours for secondary teachers) and in another report HMI commented

> *By one route or another something around 10 per cent of non-contact time is needed. Without it many primary schools, particularly small ones, will be unable to implement fully the National Curriculum and its related assessment and reporting.*
>
> (HMI, 1991)

It is against this discouraging background that the assessment coordinator has to operate and to try and convince sometimes less than enthusiastic colleagues that good assessment practice is vital in the establishment of an effective curriculum. The assessment coordinator has no better weapon than the excellent quote from the Dearing's report that recognised past mistakes and wrote

> *Records should be useful, manageable, easy to keep and easy to interpret. It is not possible for teachers to record all their knowledge and they should not be tempted to try.*

This message should be broadcast to your colleagues because it can remove a great deal of prejudice about assessment. '*It is not possible to assess everything and nor should teachers try*'. The quote should be on a flip chart in every staff room and at the front of all assessment courses. It provides clarity to the term '*minimalistic*'. Teachers should, therefore, be realistic in their approach to assessing pupils' progress and certainly be more focused on just what it is they should be looking at and recording.

So what should teachers assess? As is clear from the above, certainly not what teachers were being asked to attempt before Dearing. If assessment policy and practice is to conform to these principles, it has to be manageable. This means you should prioritise the three core subjects that are seen by the profession as being the key purpose of primary education. The simple statement on the left is used successfully to aid manageability in many schools.

Assessment of pupils' attainment should include English AT2, AT3 (reading and writing); maths AT2, AT3 (number and measures for KS1 and 2) and AT4 (data handling for KS2); and science AT1 (Experimental and investigative science).

Suggestion

Establish with all concerned on which areas of the curriculum to concentrate over a set period and in what order. In other words, create a timetable whilst keeping the process useful, manageable and easy to interpret.

Such a selection fits well with the current attention to literacy and numeracy but each school will have to make decisions such as this in the light of their own circumstances. It will be central to your school policy to gain agreement and to attain a focus for the assessment processes you will want to develop.

## 3: Gathering evidence should be simple and straightforward

How shall we gather the evidence in order to assess pupils' attainment?

It is not necessary to make special arrangements to make many of the necessary assessments as teachers already have samples of children's work, much of it referenced against the Programmes of Study (PoS) in the three core subjects. Consider, for example, the work contained in:

- nursery scrap books;
- reading records/home reading files;
- current baseline assessments/profiles;
- assessment sheets that are dated and annotated with background information;
- SAT examinations;
- individual teacher year group notes that are often kept in planning/assessment files;
- photographs;
- portfolios — school, year or class;
- tape recordings of children's conversations and/or work — e.g. non-narrative accounts.

Gathering evidence is a whole school issue and one that requires a systematic approach if there is to be uniformity and clear understanding. It is not the sole task of just one or two teachers (usually Years 2 and 6). Clear coordination guidance should lead to whole school consensus to benefit from existing school practice. The evidence of participants during courses run by the authors is that the following items are all important areas for gathering information.

## Keeping and annotating children's work

Keeping samples of pupils' work is standard practice in many primary schools, but often the process needs to be more systematic and clearly structured. A proportion of the work needs to be referenced against the Programmes of Study and some against the Level Descriptors. Schools need to have a unified structure in place to ensure that they use such materials. The assessment coordinator should be clear that good practice in this area should lead to teachers referencing to set national criteria and then, as a matter of course, level the assessed work. The format of such annotation can be seen in Chapter 7.

## Work in nursery scrapbooks

These are similar in practice to individual class portfolios. Teachers find it useful to start with a whole-class book and then quickly move on to individual child references. This frequently continues into Year 1. Such collections can contain individual children's work if the teacher feels that it is relevant to that particular child's progress. Figure 1.1 Shows children making up stories, sorting, counting and listening.

Remember '*professional responsibility is being handed back to the classroom practitioner*' (Dearing, DES, 1995). It is now up to schools to decide what records they will keep. Therefore professional responsibility is to the fore.

 *Decisions about how to mark work and record progress are professional matters for schools to consider, in the context of the needs of their children* (SCAA, 1996, pp. 7–8)

## Keeping up to date reading records

An essential part of the role of a classteacher is to keep individual reading records of the children in their care. Most feel that it is fundamental to the ongoing monitoring of achievement in the classroom. Reading records should be included as an active form of assessment. As schools develop their practices in line with the National Literacy Strategy, recording will become more structured and formal and added to these records should be any home reading records that teachers use to gather evidence regarding reading attainment and habits.

# We make up stories.

FIG 1.1
Children making up stories, sorting, counting and listening

# We listen to each other.

# Looking at the number to 'read' the price.

'Next term Kevin, who is five-and-a-half, will be formally assessed as to whether he can distinguish his phonemes from his graphemes. Depending on the result he will be streamed. If research is anything to go by, there is an 88 per cent chance he'll remain in that stream for the remainder of his school career'

(Dixon, 1997)

## Completing and then analysing Baseline profiles

Baseline profiles, an example of which is shown in Figure 1.2 (pp. 20–1), have recently been developed and should provide you with a means of measuring progress as children pass through the school. From the beginning of the autumn term in the 1998–99 school year all maintained primary schools have had to adopt a baseline assessment scheme accredited by the Qualifications and Curriculum Authority (QCA). Thus teachers have had to assess all new 4–5-year-old pupils within seven weeks of starting primary school. The assessment covers, as a minimum, the basic skills of speaking and listening, reading, writing, mathematics and personal and social development. Classteachers will from now on be able to use the information from the baseline assessments to plan their teaching to meet individual children's needs. Over time, schools will be able to judge children's progress against this baseline and schools themselves will be judged by the progress these pupils make.

It is an important feature of the scheme that headteachers have to give parents the opportunity to discuss the results of their children's assessments. Schools must also pass on the assessment results to the local education authority, who in turn will pass the information on to the Qualifications and Curriculum Authority (QCA). When a pupil changes school, his/her baseline assessment results have to be sent to the new school.

However, using such information positively may take some skill and persuasion for there is every chance that grading children so early in their school careers may have the opposite effect to raising standards. Indeed recent reports show that the effect on boys may be quite pronounced. 'Thousands of boys about to start school are in danger of being written off in their first term', writes Ghourt (1998) quoting research from LEAs and early years experts.

 *The odds are stacked against boys from the start. There is a real danger teachers will identify whole cohorts as failures. Writing them off before they've had a chance.*

Croll and Moses (1985) research on teachers' perceptions of children with reading difficulties showed that they saw these children's problems as a reflection of their inherent limitations as learners. The teachers were not generally hopeful that the additional help such pupils were receiving would make much difference.

On a wider front Good and Brophy (1991) found that those children graded as 'low achievers'

- were allowed less time by their teachers to answer questions;
- were told the answers when uncertain rather than being given prompts and hints;
- less frequently received praise;
- were spoken to in less warm, more anxious tones;
- received less informative feedback when they asked questions;
- received less eye-contact and other non-verbal communication; and,
- experienced less acceptance and their ideas were used less.

Thus one important issue for discussion between the staff is how such baseline information can be used in such a way that teachers do not treat some children as sheep and others as goats and exemplify some of the characteristics above. You may wish to use the boxes on this page to begin the discussion.

---

In Durham, for example, of the 6.732 children assessed, twice as many boys as girls fell into the bottom attainment category, failing to reach accepted standards. Girls outnumbered boys by about 30 per cent in the top group.

In number work 35 per cent of girls reached higher levels, compared to 29 per cent of boys.

---

Its no surprise that girls score higher. It has nothing to do with intelligence, boys simply develop at different rates. By Key Stage 3 this has balanced out but that might be too late for boys branded as failures — disaffection sets in early.

(Madeline Portwood, Educational Psychologist Durham County Council.)

---

Our baseline assessments are used for diagnostic purposes and to celebrate the achievements of children rather than to highlight their failures. The system has become part of our early-years classroom routine and so should not be regarded as a formal assessment of children's ability.

This systematic assessment is a better way of matching activities appropriate to each individual child's needs rather than letting teachers make early assumptions about pupils' abilities and so missing out on providing them with the most rewarding experiences and challenges'.

(Pauline Gates — Early Years Coordinator, Darton Primary School)

The information obtained from such a baseline profile, as that shown in Figure 1.2, informs the classteacher of her future teaching content and also affects the groupings within the class. Baseline profiles also allow the school to see the relative attainment of the whole cohort — their new intake.

**Barnsley Baseline Profile — established 1997**

| | | | | | | | | | | | | | | | | |
|---|---|---|---|---|---|---|---|---|---|---|---|---|---|---|---|---|
| **Social development** | | | | | | | | | | | | | | | | |
| 1 | yet to develop/be observed | *Interaction* | | | | | | | | | | | | | | |
| 2 | observes others rather than participating | | | | | | | | | | | | | | | |
| 3 | usually chooses to work/play along | | | | | | | | | | | | | | | |
| 4 | engages in parallel activity with others | | 4 | | | | | | | | | | | | | |
| 5 | engages in co-operative activity with others; shares and takes turns | | | | | | | | | | | | | | | |
| 1 | yet to develop/be observed | *Concentration* | | | | | | | | | | | | | | |
| 2 | very short attention span | | | | | | | | | | | | | | | |
| 3 | attention span limited with directed tasks | | | | | | | | | | | | | | | |
| 4 | generally concentrates well with directed and non-directed tasks | | | | | | | | | | | | | | | |
| 5 | consistently concentrates until activity concluded | | 5 | | | | | | | | | | | | | |
| 1 | yet to develop/be observed | *Motivation* | | | | | | | | | | | | | | |
| 2 | always needs an adult to start on a task | | | | | | | | | | | | | | | |
| 3 | selects own tasks; will engage on a favourite task or activity without an adult | | | | | | | | | | | | | | | |
| 4 | actively engages in a variety of tasks without adult direction | | | | | | | | | | | | | | | |
| 5 | asks many questions; interested in most tasks | | 5 | | | | | | | | | | | | | |
| **Physical development** | | | | | | | | | | | | | | | | |
| 1 | yet to develop/be observed | *Fine Motor* | | | | | | | | | | | | | | |
| 2 | always needs an adult on start on a task | | | | | | | | | | | | | | | |
| 3 | uses pincer grasp; handles small objects | | | | | | | | | | | | | | | |
| 4 | uses small tools and equipment purposefully e.g. scissors | | | | | | | | | | | | | | | |
| 5 | uses small tools and equipment with control | | 5 | | | | | | | | | | | | | |
| 1 | yet to develop/be observed | *Gross Motor* | | | | | | | | | | | | | | |
| 2 | moves confidently with coordination/awareness of others | | | | | | | | | | | | | | | |
| 3 | uses range of small/large toys with purposes | | | | | | | | | | | | | | | |
| 4 | uses range of small and large toys with purpose and control | | | | | | | | | | | | | | | |
| 5 | shows coordination in running, catching, balance, throwing, kicking, hopping | | 5 | | | | | | | | | | | | | |
| **English** | | | | | | | | | | | | | | | | |
| 1 | yet to develop/be observed | *EN1 Speaking* | | | | | | | | | | | | | | |
| 2 | uses sounds and/or gestures to communicate meaning | | | | | | | | | | | | | | | |
| 3 | speaks to peers and adults | | | | | | | | | | | | | | | |
| 4 | initiates conversation with peers and adults | | | | | | | | | | | | | | | |
| 5 | conveys simple meaning audibly and can extend accounts with detail (L1) | | 5 | | | | | | | | | | | | | |

| | | | | | | | | | | | | | | | | | | |
|---|---|---|---|---|---|---|---|---|---|---|---|---|---|---|---|---|---|---|
| 1 | yet to develop/be observed | *EN1 Listening* | | | | | | | | | | | | | | | | |
| 2 | responds to action stories/songs/rhymes | | | | | | | | | | | | | | | | | |
| 3 | listens attentively to short stories | | | | | | | | | | | | | | | | | |
| 4 | follows a two-step instruction | | | | | | | | | | | | | | | | | |
| 5 | listens to others and usually responds appropriately: takes simple messages (LI) | 5 | | | | | | | | | | | | | | | | |
| 1 | yet to develop/be observed | *EN2 Reading* | | | | | | | | | | | | | | | | |
| 2 | shows some interest in books | | | | | | | | | | | | | | | | | |
| 3 | recognises that books have a purpose | | | | | | | | | | | | | | | | | |
| 4 | recognises that print conveys meaning | 4 | | | | | | | | | | | | | | | | |
| 5 | recognises individual words and letters in familiar context (LI) | | | | | | | | | | | | | | | | | |
| 1 | yet to develop/be observed | *EN3 Writing* | | | | | | | | | | | | | | | | |
| 2 | uses pictures and/or marks to communicate | | | | | | | | | | | | | | | | | |
| 3 | uses symbols and/or individual letters to communicate meaning | | | | | | | | | | | | | | | | | |
| 4 | writes single words without a model | 4 | | | | | | | | | | | | | | | | |
| 5 | communicates meaning through simple written words and phrases (LI) | | | | | | | | | | | | | | | | | |
| **Mathematics** | | | | | | | | | | | | | | | | | | |
| 1 | yet to develop/be observed | *MA1 Using and Applying* | | | | | | | | | | | | | | | | |
| 2 | matches simple objects | | | | | | | | | | | | | | | | | |
| 3 | sorts using own attribute/s | | | | | | | | | | | | | | | | | |
| 4 | uses equipment and matches knowledge to solve a task, with help | 4 | | | | | | | | | | | | | | | | |
| 5 | decides how to tackle a task and talks about what she/he has found using mathematics as an integral part of activities (LI) | | | | | | | | | | | | | | | | | |
| 1 | yet to develop/be observed | *MA2 Number* | | | | | | | | | | | | | | | | |
| 2 | can say numbers to at least 5 | | | | | | | | | | | | | | | | | |
| 3 | uses counting equipment: counts sets 1:1 to at least 5 | | | | | | | | | | | | | | | | | |
| 4 | recognises numbers 1–10: counts and orders to 10: adds to 5 using apparatus | 4 | | | | | | | | | | | | | | | | |
| 5 | counts, orders, adds and subtracts numbers in problems involving up to 10 objects. Writes numbers (LI) | | | | | | | | | | | | | | | | | |
| 1 | yet to develop/be observed | *MA2 Algebra* | | | | | | | | | | | | | | | | |
| 2 | copies patterns of two colours or objects | | | | | | | | | | | | | | | | | |
| 3 | continues a pattern using 2 colours or objects | | | | | | | | | | | | | | | | | |
| 4 | continues a pattern using 3 or 4 colours or objects | 4 | | | | | | | | | | | | | | | | |
| 5 | recognises and devises repeating patterns, counting the numbers in each repeat (LI) | | | | | | | | | | | | | | | | | |
| 1 | yet to develop/be observed | *MA3 Shape and Space* | | | | | | | | | | | | | | | | |
| 2 | sorts square, rectangle, triangle, circle by shape | | | | | | | | | | | | | | | | | |
| 3 | recognises and names square, rectangle, triangle, circle | | | | | | | | | | | | | | | | | |
| 4 | understands words commonly used to describe simple properties of space and shape | 4 | | | | | | | | | | | | | | | | |
| 5 | uses everyday language to describe 2D and 3D properties and positions (LI) | | | | | | | | | | | | | | | | | |

© Barnsley Advisory Support and Inspection Service

FIG 1.2
Entry and baseline assessment

## Getting children to complete assessment sheets that are dated and annotated with background information

These sheets should be used across the school and give National Curriculum level information, standardised scores and any background. Teachers should be encouraged to date the work and to give some reasoning for their choice of level. An example of this could be:

> This is a piece of non-narrative writing — a first draft of Michael's visit to the Imperial War Museum in connection with Year 6 work on Britain since the 1930s. This is a piece of work that has been looked at by Mike Wintle and Mrs K Smith and given a level 3 because . . . The account displays at least half of the sentences have been demarcated. The style of writing shows a number of simple connectives such as 'but' and 'because'. The text is organised by a series of points and there is evidence of some attention to detail.

> We went to the Imepiel War Museum today and we looked at really good things. We saw planes on the roof they were hanging by rope and we thought they would fall on us. The best bit was the blitz hut. It felt as if we were really there. It was cool we all felt frightened but I was glad my teacher was with us. I like her. The trench that we walked in smelt bad and I saw a wounded soldier lying in a dugout it looked like he had been shot. His leg was bleeding. We were glad to leave the trench. I enjoyed my day and would like to go back again.

## SATs

SAT results are the most significant performance indicator used by inspectors, parents and other professionals. This is a simple fact of life and one that has to be accepted by all members of staff whether they like it or not. Nationally the results of SATs differ very little from teacher assessments but in any individual school, tests are likely to be taken more seriously. Therefore, they are another element of the jigsaw that makes up the monitoring procedures albeit not without problems.

*Teachers have found that the distinction between SAT scores of one, two, three are too broad, and open to misinterpretation for effective diagnoses. The scores fail to discriminate effectively between pupils, making any judgments about standards between schools or between pupils from one year to another*

> *uncertain. For teachers, therefore, the work involved seems*
> *highly disproportionate in relation to the perceived benefits'*
>
> (Galton, 1995, p. 57)

Gathering such results has now been made simple in Key
Stage 2. It is a paper exercise. Analysing them is a more
difficult process and time has to be found for assessment
coordinators and their headteachers to prepare the material
for presentation to subject coordinators. (Chapter 5)

## Teacher observation and notes

Many teachers keep notes of their children's achievements,
normally in their planning or assessment files or mark books.
These are then used at parents' evenings, and are useful when
writing reports or when children are assessed for the special
needs register. The content of these notes can be varied and
cover vast areas of knowledge — anything from mathematics
levels, behavioural issues, to whether the child needs to
improve on their handwriting.

## Individual education plans (IEPs)

The Special Needs Code of Practice requires schools to set up
Individual Educational Plans (IEPs). Children's needs have to
be reviewed with the parents on a regular basis. To meet these
needs teacher and child should set specific learning targets
such as those discussed in the chapter on target setting. The
success criteria and named people are all agreed and written
down. Such information should not be overlooked when
considering the data available to school management when
considering priorities.

## Portfolios

Headteachers will need to show evidence in order to support
their judgments about the standards of pupils' attainment
within their schools and demonstrate the accuracy of
judgments made by teachers in assessing pupils' National
Curriculum levels. Portfolios are ideal tools for schools to
gather this evidence and demonstrate judgments in a
manageable form (see Chapter 6 on portfolios).

**Suggestion**

Discuss with the headteacher the benefits if the school were to purchase a cheap camera with a zoom lens. Issue all coordinators with a file in which to keep the photographic evidence. Teachers' Centres may be able to lend you a video camera and a digital camera would allow you to store and display such pictures in computer files.

**Suggestion**

Produce the list of your own school's current assessment processes and practices. This could be used right at the start of the consideration of assessment when you are preparing the ground for the headteacher.

Open a whole school debate on the desired degree of formal testing in Key Stage 2 — for example, using NFER material, draw up a suggested format covering such matters as when they will take place and where the children will undertake them and the areas to be tested. What use will be made of the results? Will you test in maths / English / reading?

## Taking photographs and videos

Photographs and videos are simple and effective ways of recording lesson content and showing examples of children's work. They may be particularly useful when compiling summative reports of children's attainment in using and applying mathematics, speaking and listening in English and experimenting in science. Video also has a use in considering performance in art, physical education, technology and IT.

For schools preparing for an internal review or external examination, such as an OFSTED inspection, the use of pre-recorded material is an excellent way of extending the snapshot and allowing the school to show off its achievements. The history coordinator could, for example, go into classrooms after school once a week and record the development of the topics, the PE coordinator might record the way in which dance progresses across the year. Such evidence gathering is good practice and will include work both in the classroom and from school displays. Photographs need to be kept throughout both Key Stage 1 and Key Stage 2. They are useful tools for showing governors what is actually going on in school and can be used as background at meetings of the governing body.

# 4: Assessments need to be systematic and timely

## How often should we assess?

| | |
|---|---|
| **Formal teacher assessment** | This should occur in all three core subjects once a year |
| **Informal assessment** | This is again in maths, English and science and should be a minimum of three times per subject per term |
| **School examinations and periodic tests** | School exams should happen once per year, Periodic tests obviously periodically |
| **End of Key Stage assessments** | Once a year at the end of Years 2 and 6 |
| **Records of Achievement** | These should be ongoing and usually updated each half term |

**_Suggestion_**

Establish with the Maths and Science coordinators a bank of attainment target tasks that can be completed in the current school setting.

School-wide assessment needs to be systematic, otherwise pupils' development cannot be shown, putting the whole exercise into jeopardy. If time and effort is spent in one year on one aspect and this is not followed up later, the earlier effort has been wasted. Systematic assessment might, for example, show poor attainment for boys in En3, right through the junior phase. It might help to pinpoint where the problem is more acute and suggest remedies to the situation.

The assessment overview shown in Figure 1.3 is what is now attempted at Darton Primary School in Barnsley. It is condensed to a single sheet of paper and can be understood easily, making for simplicity for whole-school staff meetings and a useful way to highlight how much assessment actually goes on.

The key area of concern in schools within the informal stages of pupil assessment is the interpretation of the informal results. Any interpretation of children's work needs to be listed against agreed references (for example Level Descriptors from the National Curriculum).

Assessment needs to be timely for it to be useful, manageable and for it to be undertaken properly. It will need a purposeful and determined assessment coordinator to make it so. Assessment needs to happen at regular intervals in order to give the teacher the opportunity to determine future teaching, but it should never dominate the classroom as has been the case in the past. The whole process resembles a very complicated balancing act. The above schedule means that ATs in English, maths and science are formally assessed annually, which gives a total of seven assessments (if the process is started in reception) over each child's primary school career. This is more than enough to gauge and report on children's progress in ATs linked to the Programmes of Study in the National Curriculum. Informal assessments in each of the three core subjects should be undertaken three times per term.

| Assessment overview | | |
|---|---|---|
| **Teaching group** | **Year** | **All 3 core subjects** |
| **Formal teacher assessment** | Frequency | Mathematics — English — science once each |
| | Purpose | Progression |
| | Agent | School |
| | Audience | Teacher / parents |
| | Form | Various |
| **Informal teacher assessment** | Frequency | Min 3 per core |
| | Purpose | Progression |
| | Agent | School |
| | Audience | Teacher / parents |
| | Form | Record of significant achievements |
| **School examination or periodic tests** | Frequency | Once per year (usually during SAT week) |
| | Purpose | To create a school profile and for reports |
| | Agent | School |
| | Audience | Teacher, parents, governors |
| | Form | Tests |
| **End of Key Stage assessment** | Frequency | Year 2 and Year 6 |
| | Purpose | National Assessment |
| | Agent | QCA |
| | Audience | National |
| | Form | Test |
| Other assessment | | |
| **Record of Achievement** | Frequency | Ongoing (each half term) |
| | Purpose | Self assessment / celebrate achievement |
| | Agent | School |
| | Audience | School / home |
| | Form | School work / RoA folder |

© M. Wintle

FIG 1.3
Example of an assessment overview

## 5: Records of the assessment results

These records should be simple and accessible.

Mortimer's studies of what makes a school effective highlighted the need to keep and use records of pupil's progress.

 *They (headteachers) also influence the teaching strategies of teachers, but only selectively, where they judged it necessary. The leadership was demonstrated by an emphasis on the monitoring of pupils' progress, through teachers keeping individual records. Approaches varied — some schools kept written records; others passed on folders of pupils' work to their next teacher; some did both — but a systematic policy of record keeping was important.* (Mortimer et al., 1993, p. 11)

How shall we record what we find out about children's achievements? The type of record needs to be appropriate for both the method used to make the assessment, and the content of what is assessed. The way in which record keeping meets the needs of assessment and serves the purposes of the process as a whole is going to be a key indicator of the manageability of the task. It therefore has to be right. Many of the records kept will be annotations of the product itself as outlined in the previous section. Others will be such things as mark lists. Indeed if you have ever been asked to develop a structure for recording evidence of assessment, the finished article will probably look suspiciously like a mark book! The process undertaken for recording table tests, spelling, comprehension marks etc., are daily/weekly forms of assessment and practising teachers simply call it by another name — marking.

Experience has shown that early progress can be made by the coordinator when whole staff come together to discuss their current practice. The result could be something like the following list:

| *What is being assessed and how* | *The records kept* |
|---|---|
| Weekly routines such as tables/spelling tests | These can be kept in teachers' mark books |
| Teacher observation: these could be how a child deals with the tasks set, especially in investigative AT1 work. Observations are enhanced and far more focused if there are set criteria to measure against (see Chapter 4). | These form their own record, for example, 'can do's' in reading or AT1 science available to check against the child's progress. This not only makes the whole process of assessing children's work far more manageable but actually knowing before the activity was to be assessed simply makes the process far more acceptable and in practical terms far easier to cope with. |
| Examining product evidence | Children's finished product is by far the largest part of a record keeping system. It needs, however, to be referenced to the Programmes of Study. |
| Discussions with children: as individuals or/and in small groups This should include the reading and writing conferences. | Useful evidence can be kept as notes in mark books or in reading records. |
| Teacher intervention in small groups | Ongoing files such as portfolios and teachers' notes. |
| Marking to an agreed policy A simple policy can erase all the seemingly minor problems such as should staff mark in red or is it right to mark with a child present. A marking policy is offered as a working example in Chapter 9. | Children keep the results of teachers' marking in their work books of course, but if scores are given or if anything noteworthy is found then mark books are the place to record. |
| Listening to children read | Listening to children read is an obvious form of assessment and should be viewed by all staff as an integral part of an ongoing rigorous child assessment practice. With the advent of group reading in the literacy hour, however, others will now need to listen to individuals read and schools will need to find a way to incorporate their assessments into their ongoing informal assessment practices. |
| Using assessment material produced by both the school or purchased from commercial sources | Many mathematics schemes have excellent assessment material and provide a package of simple recording pages for teachers to use at will. These tests make the whole process manageable, relevant and simple to use. It also links in with the ongoing curriculum, with frequent assessment that is used properly pointing the way to future teaching. |
| Screening packages that can be administered within the school's agreed assessment policy This recorded assessment data used alongside teacher assessment provides an all round data gathering process of pupil progress. | The results obtained can be kept in teachers' assessment folders. |
| Other assessments such as SAT results, this also will include SAT practise papers especially in the Years 5 and 6. | The results obtained can be kept in teachers' assessment folders. |

## 6: Children's involvement in assessment

Children should be involved in the assessment of their own work and progress.

Educational gains will be accelerated the closer children are to the assessment of their own work. This is more than GAAMY (go away and mark it yourself), it involves an understanding and acceptance of the targets set for the lesson, the half term, the year, and a growing ability by children to make judgments about their own progress. Such development is part of the social, moral, spiritual and cultural development (which teachers usually call personal development) as judged by OFSTED. Self-assessment is important and the coordinator will do well to emphasise this to staff in briefing sessions and staff room discussions.

Alison Standing (1998) headteacher of Rodmell Primary School, describes the way this principle has helped turn her school around from one requiring 'special measures'.

 *Children are involved in evaluating their own work and with teachers stating clearly what they want the children to learn and why, the activity is given purpose and direction. Procedures for assessing pupils' performance now require us to relate the outcomes of children's work to the original intention.*

(p. 36)

How can children be involved in judgments about their own work and progress?

| | |
|---|---|
| What assessments can children make of their own work and progress? | Marking their own work when appropriate, 'opting' to complete check sheets or take progress tests when they think they are ready. Working on computer programs which keep a file of achievement and annotating the printout stating the progress since last time. Creating, completing and updating Records of Achievement (RoA). |
| When should these be undertaken? | Periodic checks and tests can be made both by the teacher and by the child under his or her volition. The RoA ought to be every half term or term depending on the format of the record and the work currently being undertaken. |
| How can they be trained to do this? | Firstly by encouraging children to read and act upon the comments about their work made by others, and then by getting them to reply appropriately to those comments (creating a dialogue). By constant practise and guided child self-selection of material for the RoA. |

This principle is more easily achieved if the school has an established whole-school teaching and learning policy. This should include the objective that children be given systematic opportunities to regularly self-assess their own work and practice. In the best teaching, lessons start with the purpose of the activity being explained to the class. Thus pupils are told not only what they are to do but why are they are doing it; who is the work for; and, what they will learn by the activity. In the plenary session at the end of each teaching activity, children are brought together as a group and given the chance to discuss their work and how well they feel things have been going. This gives children an excellent chance to assess their work process and indeed decide on whether or not they've achieved any personal targets. When lessons conclude in this manner they provide opportunities for regular, ongoing self-assessment and target setting. This lesson structure is the one recommended by the National Numeracy Project.

As confirmed supporters of Records of Achievements, we've been impressed just how useful this form of assessment can be in increasing the quality of learning for young children. RoA will be discussed in detail in another chapter but there need to be systems that are:

- both termly and ongoing to provide a consistency of practice especially when the system is first established in school.
- clear in how RoA will work and explicit as towards how much the initiative will cost both in time and money, both to set-up and in ongoing expenses.
- very clear in the role of pupils' self-assessment and future target-setting.

The school can also usefully link RoA with areas of its discipline policy or house/pastoral systems (see Chapter 7).

## 7: Assessment and classroom organisation

The demands of assessment should enhance good classroom organisation not hinder it.

Teaching which maximises the contact between pupils and teacher will affect the progress children make. Such contact is also, of course, the route to good quality assessment. What kind of classroom organisation should we seek? Proctor, Entwistle, Judge and McKenzie-Murdoch (1995) discuss this issue as follows:

*In most situations it is totally unrealistic to expect to assess all the children in your class at any one time. Who you choose to assess at any one particular moment is inseparable from how you manage and organise your classroom and how and whether you group children. . . . you need to think carefully about how you wish to assess and what assessment techniques you wish to deploy when you select the particular teaching style and classroom organisation for a particular teaching/ learning session.* (pp. 115–16)

Both assessment and teaching share common needs for well considered classroom organisation.

- It is important that the teaching style fits the intended learning outcome and therefore the task and teachers' planning should identify a teaching style.
- Classroom organisation should encourage and foster independent learning. For instance do children know where the materials are kept? Are they labelled and accessible?
- Staff should identify a clear role for the classroom assistant/parental helper in their everyday lessons but also particularly when they are attempting to assess AT1 maths, science and English.
- Seating arrangements may reflect prior attainment, friendship groups or behavioural needs. These may change from subject to subject and for independent study work other arrangements altogether might be more suitable. When periodic assessments are taking place yet other classroom arrangements may be needed, but this will be more easily accomplished if children are used to a variety of settings.

A number of questions need to be asked:

**Do all staff understand the content that they have to teach** and further do they understand the different pedagogical demands of different subjects? Mathematics is not just reading with numbers; gaining an understanding of chronology involves different thinking processes from learning about making a fair test! We might therefore expect to see (in planning files) an acknowledgment that different demands are satisfied in different ways.

**How are different teachers' classrooms organised to foster pupils' independent learning?** Some messages to the education service from various official sources may tend to encourage teachers to adopt inappropriate teaching strategies borrowed from other cultures where promoting independence is not valued. You might wish to ask — Are resources arranged to promote children's own independence? Are children encouraged to sort out their own scissors, crayons and are resources clearly marked? Are children given the opportunity to suggest ideas to teachers and to each other?

**Has the role of the classroom assistant (NTA), nursery nurse or parental helper been properly addressed?** The use of additional voluntary or paid staff can make a difference to the manageability and quality of assessment, especially when dealing with AT1 science, maths and English. It is important to utilise these areas of adult help and expertise because, at the very least, teachers have to be free to monitor AT1 whilst the others are usefully occupied. This arrangement is part of good teaching — target groups in the literacy hour, work with IT peripherals, for example, make this organisational demand. Having adult help in the classroom helps to conquer the organisation of problems of difficult assessment activities, as long as the tasks that the rest of the children are undertaking are low in teacher input.

**Is there good quality classroom organisation that fosters ongoing teacher assessment?** For example, do children sit in rows or groups? This has an effect on a whole range of matters from teacher input time to real group work. Ask yourself, and your colleagues, the reasoning behind children sitting in groups when the activities being undertaken are designed for individuals. All too often seating in classrooms does not facilitate the way children work. For example, when discussing whole-staff agreement on a curriculum issue, staff will sit in a group debating and influencing the content. If the task is an individual one, for example, writing a report on your subject for the governor's curriculum committee, then you will probably sit alone at a desk. You need to encourage a match between room organisation and the tasks required. Moving the room around takes only minutes to accomplish and has real implications for our children's work practices. This may prove difficult to many colleagues who believe in 'all children sitting all day in groups', which may be suitable for 'real group work' activities, but when individual work is desired such a classroom layout may be less appropriate. Thus good quality ongoing teacher assessment needs a classroom organisation that supports individual work, just as the work itself does.

## 8: Assessment practices and equal opportunities

Assessment practices should contribute towards the achievement of equal opportunities. What provisions are there currently to promote equal opportunities?

When starting to build a whole-school assessment policy intended to lead to systematic planning for assessment, equal opportunities issues need to be addressed. Coordinators may be fortunate to find that these are already in place. Such schools will have:

- the identification of principles of equal opportunities in all policy documents;
- an equal opportunities policy in place with positive action going on;
- a special needs policy that complies with the Code of Practice;
- appropriate differentiation in the classroom both by task content and outcome;
- assessment practices that give all children the opportunity to show what they know.

Indeed this is exactly what a whole-school assessment policy strives to achieve rather than a series of simple tasks that lead children to being 'tripped up' because of poor planning or ill-thought out assessment.

An example of how the development of a good equal opportunities approach can affect assessment practice is shown in the interest in reading materials shown by boys and girls. Thus teachers will need to take account, when assessing boys' reading levels, not only of the material which will help them to come to a professional judgment but also choose material which will interest boys. This frequently means not just stories but books with a factual / technological bias. More fundamentally EOs must mean that we frame our policies, our arguments, our practices with the aim to challenge or displace

**Winston Churchill**
*I should like to have been asked what I knew. They always tried to ask what I did not know. When I would willingly have displayed my knowledge they sought to expose my ignorance.* (quoted in Daily Telegraph, 3.9.85)

**What does equal opportunities mean?**
Operating a policy of equal opportunities means offering the same encouragement, support, consideration, care and experiences of teaching and learning to everyone...
(Darton Primary School EO policy)

## Suggestion

Make sure that you are aware of the content and status of your school's equal opportunities policy. Review with concerned staff, and determine how systematic tracking through regular pupil assessment can help in monitoring its operation.

the ideas that individuals are endowed with a fixed ability which will determine the upper limit of their potential for learning (Hart, 1998) This means in practice re-examining the effects of 'setting' or streaming by encouraging movement between groups; giving value to all types of pupil by encouraging movement between groups; giving value to all groups of school activity at which different children excel; and preventing the 'labelling' of pupils because of a test; an observation; a SAT result, or worse, a baseline test on entry.

## 9: Issues of access

The intended access to children's records should be known before anything is written. Demands for access to the results you have gathered will abound.

> Demands from LEAs for monitoring purposes, from head-teachers, for the production of records of achievement, for reports to parents . . . transfer information for receiving schools, for OFSTED and for researchers have to be met.
>
> (Shipman, 1993)

This places additional burdens on schools but the worst scenario would be for the effort in gathering all that information to be wasted as the files lie dormant in the office. It needs to be used to inform as many people as appropriate.

Who will have access to the children's records?
- The parents have a legal right to view their own child(ren)'s records.
- Governors will see the results of assessments (but not those of individual pupils).
- Records will not only need to show what levels each child is on but also the content to which this applies and how the assessment was made: test / classwork etc.?
- All staff will need to be familiar with rights to access for records.

Children's records can be seen as a right by their own parents. This places an even greater onus on those who compile the records to be accurate, fair and to confine comments to those accurately reflecting pupils' achievements and progress. It also implies that some explanations may be needed about the levels (pupils are expected to make a gain of one level every two years — not one as some believe).

Governors will see the results of assessments (but not those of individual pupils) as they should as the body charged with *'holding the school to account'* (OFSTED, 1994). Those of us with a long-term investment in the education system are prepared for the fluctuation of scores year by year depending on staffing, intake and curriculum changes. Not so governors (and many parents) who are sensitised by rising / falling standards rhetoric and consequently may be very quick to judge. The schools' senior management team need to prepare governors for such news. This again relies on accurate tracking methods for each cohort as they move through the school: in short, having good assessment practices, policies and records.

A simple tick-sheet may disguise the fact that different assessments are carried out in different ways and at very different times. The standards achieved by individuals in tests compared to normal classroom conditions may vary considerably; at various times in the year, in the week, of the day, we perform differently. The times and context of the assessment need to be part of the record and especially with a variety of audiences, a balance struck between too much information and a simple description of context.

In this age of increased accountability and community rights, teachers and others in the school need to be aware of just who has the right to view pupils' records (and the sometimes quite personal comments made on a particular child). As coordinator you need to know that parents can demand to see what has been written regarding their child, and your school is therefore required to set up systems that can deal with this increasing demand.

All the following have some kinds of access to children's records:
■ parents and guardians;
■ governors;
■ staff;
■ the LEA.

At Darton Primary School, for example, the targets for the number of Year 6 pupils reaching level four in the core subjects were set through wide discussion between parents, governors and staff. This was only possible because the staff have to hand systematically recorded accurate and intelligible assessment data about each child; governors had been part of the policy setting process; and parents were used to seeing, discussing and working with their children to achieve targets. Children's personal targets thus contributed to a realistic definition of the overall goal.

Schools need to decide what information is to be given to whom. It is wise for all staff, on a regular basis, to explain to parents at parents' evenings the National Curriculum levels their children have achieved, at least in the three core subjects. Some schools have also started the system of agreeing with parents their child's improvement targets in the three core subjects in English, maths and science. The staff should be brought to view this as part of home/school partnerships.

## 10: Parents' and governors' involvement in assessment

Parents and governors should be involved in the creation and monitoring of the assessment policy.

> *The progress charted on each child can be used not only by the teacher to help the child, but to involve the parents'.* They will discuss the results they receive with teachers. *'That is a short step from encouraging them to see and discuss detailed progress sheets on which the report is based. This promises a wealth of information as a base for cooperation over learning between teacher, child and parent.* (Shipman, 1993, p. 65)

How can parents and governors be involved?
- Parental/governor involvement in making up the assessment policy.
- Parental/governor involvement in agreement trialling.
- Targeting parental help in classroom management especially while assessment tasks are taking place.
- Opportunities for parents to view child's records showing attainment and progress referenced to NC levels.
- Parent evenings where assessment and level descriptors are discussed.
- Governor discussion and feedback during governor curriculum meetings.

If teachers are serious about parents being involved in all aspects of school life then they should be actively concerned with the way pupils are assessed and the policy for the gathering, analysis and use to which the information is put. The same applies to governors and this can be achieved through a variety of initiatives. The following expands upon these ideas.

### Parental and governor involvement with the overall assessment policy

Schools should try, wherever possible, actively to involve parents in the day to day assessment decision making of the school. This should set the ground rules for establishing the criteria for awarding National Curriculum levels.

### This leads naturally to governors and parents being involved in agreement trialling

From experience nothing helps the cause of assessment more than involving two or more governors in ongoing staff development in assessment. Your governors will come to see that there are obvious difficulties in trying to assess set pieces of work against national framework criteria and that this can be a real boost for teachers at the school. The governors for their part will develop a real empathy for the obvious difficulties that their staff have to cope with.

### Parents are able to be involved in the classroom while the teachers make AT1 maths and science assessments

This can ease the classroom teacher's burden at a very crucial time but also has important hidden issues in that parents can see the assessment process at first hand. This is crucial in the ongoing bridge-building between home and school. Furthermore, the benefits of the 'playground parliament' can be a vital part in achieving excellence. Experiences show that a parent will tell nine to ten other parents of any personal findings that they have witnessed in school. When good assessment practice, quality learning and an orderly environment has been achieved — parents who are helping the teacher become an effective form of advertising.

### Examples of levelled children's work shown at termly parents' evenings

In the past such ideas have often been rejected by teachers as many believe that parents will not understand the levelling process. We reject this idea. Parents are entitled to be told at what level their child is currently working in each of the three core subjects. This information can be taken from their ongoing significant logging sheets. It pays to educate parents in the mysteries of the National Curriculum by newsletters, 'try it' nights, open half-days and various other initiatives. Parents, whilst not professing to be expert in such fields, have a right to know. How, after all, will parents know what the next level looks like — unless you tell them? It is, of course, also incumbent on teachers to try to continue their termly ongoing assessments.

**Governor discussion on assessment matters**

This is usually done during the termly curriculum committee meetings and then communicated to the full governing body. This has obvious benefits:

- governors' knowledge increases about ongoing assessment initiatives;
- governors can have a significant input into practice. This could include governors not only discussing assessment practice for the coming term but also agreeing to come into class to view ongoing assessment.
- establishing and maintaining communication between governors and staff;
- governors establishing the security of SAT papers and also seeing the children taking the tests themselves.

# 11: Reporting to parents

The results of assessments of pupils' progress should be reported regularly to parents with appropriate detail.

Since 1988 the government has made much of the fact that schools are now reporting to parents on a regular basis. Between the two authors we have 42 years of teaching, and association with many schools as governors, parents and consultants. Neither of us has ever been in a school that failed to send out such reports to parents. So this is scarcely a reform! Such good practice was already firmly established as part of the ongoing reporting to parents of a child's progress. The law now states that schools must report to parents at least once per year and that parents should have the opportunity to meet with staff and comment on the report content. Nevertheless schools have to determine the structure of such reporting. Individual schools need to decide:

- when and how often reports will be sent to parents;
- what format these reports should take? For example should the report be handwritten or use computer technology?
- if there should be a written and agreed reporting policy.

The reporting policy is part of the tripartite policy of assessment, record keeping and reporting to parents.

## When and how often will reports be sent out to parents?

Standard practice for most schools is to send reports to parents once a year, probably at the end of the summer term and usually in relation to joining these with Key Stage 1 and Key Stage 2 SAT results, the publication of which is also a legal requirement. There are variations, for example, one of the writers receives reports about his own children at least once a term. These reports are contained in an A4 booklet, and are always of a standardised nature.

Precisely when reports come out is a headteacher/staff/ governor decision and will fit in with the needs of the school, your job is to prepare the staff to meet the deadlines required.

## What format should these reports take?

Should the report be handwritten or use computer technology? A majority of parents like handwritten reports and staff want computer generated reports because they find it saves time.

| Using computer generated reports for parents | |
|---|---|
| Advantages | Disadvantages |
| Can save (some) teachers' time | takes a while to set up and for teachers to practise using the comment banks. Usually these banks need to be augmented by additional comments pertinent to the school situation — taking more time. It also frequently takes up a lot of the assessment coordinator's time (sometimes involving the IT coordinator as well). |
| Issues of spelling, grammar, handwriting are resolved — hopefully! | |
| Demonstrates a use of ICT to staff, children and parents. | |
| Teachers can be forced to address certain issues/aspects of the curriculum. | If parents within the class compared reports they would see only a limited range of comments are used. |
| Less vague and more pertinent to the PoS covered. | Can be seen as impersonal unless handwritten teacher/headteacher comments are included. |
| | Language is not moderated for different parents. |

In general computer generated reports contain far fewer generalisations such as 'likes reading' and 'could do better with his tables' because careful scrutiny of the comment banks (by you/the headteacher) prevents such phrases from inclusion. These reports are frequently more pertinent to the subject, clearly link to the National Curriculum, are more detailed and relate well to targets set and achieved within the core subjects. By restricting comments to the pre-determined PoS for each age group you will be able to ensure that as pupils progress through the school their reports reflect a progression in skills, knowledge and understanding.

## 12: Review and evaluation of the policy

Your policy document should have:
- stated policy aims with set written times for review;
- involvement of all staff;
- use of questionnaires both to parents and staff to evaluate effectiveness and fitness for purpose; and
- staffroom minutes that show staff feelings towards the workings and the practices of the evaluations of the assessment document.

It is not enough to initiate any kind of change and then leave it. Some sort of review of policies is inevitable especially in these constantly changing times. At the start of a process of establishing a whole-school assessment policy, staff and governors need to have worked out the following points:
- when the policy will be reviewed and this needs to be stated in the school's assessment document;
- how the policy will be evaluated which could take the form of
    planned and timetabled staff development meetings;
    questionnaire to staff;
    planned in-service days.

The assessment policy should be reviewed and evaluated after the first year. Once staff are familiar with the processes, and governors, parents and children are all aware of being part of it, then review periods could be expanded to once every three years.

## Evaluation

**Planned and timetabled staff meetings**

These need to be written down on a termly basis and of course this will also affect the school's development plan. One of the key areas will be to monitor the school's portfolios, and therefore agreement trialling and work levelling should be attempted at least termly. This gives staff skills and confidence in order to regularly assess and level work.

**Questionnaire to staff**

In order to obtain information, questioning staff about the relative merits of certain points of the assessment policy should take place as a means of school audit right at the beginning of the initiative. It's unlikely that a questionnaire will be needed to inform you of the staff's views on the relative merits and demerits of the existing policy. They will tell you this through discussion during normal staff meetings.

**Planned in-service days**

These are always important when setting up a whole-school assessment initiative. The benefits will be seen in the speed with which practices can be adopted and the staff's increase in understanding of the various features of good assessment. However, with the introduction of the literacy and numeracy hours the number of INSET days available means that it is unlikely that schools will find the time for whole day in-service on assessment. By considering a variety of approaches to evaluation you may well be able to fit each one into an after-school session.

Evaluation of this policy will follow the lines of those proposed by David Playfoot et al. (1989) in *The Primary School Management Book*. They identify seven approaches and interested coordinators may wish to follow a number of strands.
- structured staff discussion
- staff interviews
- work shadowing
- paired observation
- interest group sessions
- snowball sessions
- formulation of performance indicators

The following strategies will assist the smooth running of any evaluative approach.

- Why, when and what do you wish to evaluate? Who do you want to be involved? What will you do with the results?
- Be clear about the form of the feedback from any evaluation. It must be accurate and fairly stated so that staff can determine action to be taken.
- Be realistic and honest at all times. It is worth waiting a little longer in order to carry the whole team with you. Do not attempt to force issues, overstate your case, or allow your enthusiasm to cause you to mislead your colleagues.
- Seek a balanced picture where you can identify both positive and negative effects and where success and degrees of success (the word failure can usually be avoided!) can be reported.

■ Progressively focus your attention. As change takes time, so the context will alter. Some staff will be promoted and others will retire, new teachers will arrive. Roles, responsibilities and priorities will change and government initiatives will come and then be superseded. Don't allow yourself to become frustrated by the fact that your targets do not stand still. Expect redefinition of your goals, plan for the possibility of new initiatives and, where possible, use them to your advantage.

■ Use a mixture of strategies and approaches. No one method alone will do. Variety will allow everyone to contribute more fully.

■ Manage the evaluation. Sensitivity is required. Your management of the evaluation process should be deliberate. You must seek meaningful and worthwhile evaluation but always recognise that the school is run by human beings with frailties and the capacity to misjudge situations — just like we do!

By establishing the twelve principles within this chapter you may move closer towards developing the detail of practice and eventually agree a policy amongst your colleagues. The remainder of this book, whilst not intended as a blueprint for any school may provide you with a background against which the principles may be practised.

We next turn to the way in which you, as coordinator, can become more effective in establishing such practice, principles and eventually policy.

## Chapter 2      The key role of the assessment coordinator in effective primary schools

    6 *At the heart of any effective department is the effective organ-*
*isation of teaching and learning . . . (they) are also charac-*
*terised by the care and attention which they pay to the process*
*of assessment. The assessment systems of effective depart-*
*ments include . . . detailed and up to date record keeping;*
*emphasis is placed upon trying to make marking consistent;*
*efforts are made to try to give the pupils a stake in the assess-*
*ment; pupils are encouraged to discuss their marks with the*
*teacher in order to try to understand the strengths and weak-*
*nesses of their own efforts; using the assessment system as a*
*vehicle for frequent feedback to the pupils; feedback tends to*
*be criterion referenced rather than norm-referenced.*

(Harris, Jamieson and Russ, 1996, pp. 52–3)

The previous chapter set out just how central to effective
teaching and learning was good assessment practice and
several principles for its use in primary classrooms. Pupils
only get one chance in the reception class, only one chance
in Year 6. Indeed they only get one chance to learn each year
and therefore their time in school is precious. It cannot be
repeated. Effective schools do make a difference to pupil's
progress and this book argues that pupils' and teachers' time
can be better focused if teachers know what their pupils can
and cannot do, know what they did and didn't achieve last
year — and plan accordingly. This makes a school effective at
motivating its pupils, affecting their attitudes and promoting

learning. Whatever type of job description you have, this is the central role of the assessment coordinator.

The most important and influential research in this area was carried out in London in the 1980s by a team lead by Peter Mortimer. Over a number of years, they were able to isolate several features within schools which were best able to affect pupils' progress and their attitude towards school. They discovered that the twelve key factors for effective junior schooling were:

- Purposeful leadership by the headteacher
- The involvement of the deputy head
- The involvement of teachers
- Consistency amongst teachers
- Structured lessons
- Intellectually challenging teaching
- A work-centred environment
- Limited focus within sessions
- Maximum communication between teachers and pupils
- Record keeping
- Parental involvement
- A positive climate

(Mortimer, Sammons, Stoll, Lewis, and Ecob, 1988)

This list of features is echoed in this book. Some, such as the necessity for structured lessons with a limited focus (Chapter 3 on planning); the need for useful records so that pupils' time is not wasted (throughout the book); the necessity for the involvement of teachers (Chapter 4), show coordinators how to make their schools more effective in the prime task of helping pupils develop to their fullest potential. Other matters listed above should give you as coordinator ways to consider how to become more effective in developing and implementing good assessment practices in your school in line with the school's priorities.

## Why have a policy?

The essence of good practice in assessment, as in everything else, is what goes on in the classroom not what is listed on paper. As elsewhere in this series the slogan 'Practice into

Key reasons for having a policy document include:
- to guide lesson planning;
- to inform teachers and pupils what is expected of them;
- to identify resource needs; and,
- to inform INSET planning.

policy not policy into practice' is the ideal sought. The twelve principles impact on practice, this eventually is summarised in the policy.

However, whether or not your school currently has the benefit of a written assessment document, it can be argued that a de-facto policy on assessment already exists. Even if you should find that teachers are entirely free to choose whether or not to assess the core and foundation subjects; that children's self-assessment consists of giving the children mark books and letting them loose on each other's work — that amounts to a policy! If senior management are content for such practices then presumably they will not mind it being documented in a formal written policy to be given to governors, new teachers and students, inspectors and advisers. If however, these things do happen but are not desired, then your effort in pulling staff together to agree more appropriate assessment procedures and making use of such data will probably be welcomed and supported.

A whole school policy for assessment, recording and reporting (AR&R) can:
- publicly demonstrate the school's intentions for evaluation and reporting children's progress;
- help make a case for funding if commercial tests etc. are needed;
- give information to parents, governors and inspectors;
- provide information for individual teacher's planning;
- aid coherence, continuity, progression and shape priorities;
- assist in achieving uniformity and consistency in school decision making by helping to focus the minds of various decision making groups such as governors, the senior management team, other subject coordinators, toward common aims.

If a policy document exists then you have a starting point with which to compare practice; to measure up to the twelve principles and something to guide discussions with staff. If not, or if the policy bears no relation to reality, then sooner or later you will need to begin the process of working with your teacher colleagues to create one which does.

The policy document will need to show the mechanisms in place that the school has to:
- stay informed of developments, both technical and curricular;
- develop the curriculum in the light of those changes;
- resource any subsequent needs;
- keep staff skills up to date.

A written whole-school assessment policy needs to be owned by the whole staff, describe what is actually happening in classrooms and give some indication of the direction the school is going with regard to the collection and use of assessment data. If in its construction teachers become a little more aware about how other teachers are assessing pupils' achievements and how they are using the information, then a more coherent approach may well evolve without you having to do very much at all.

Whole school policies for assessment, reporting and marking (see Chapter 9) can publicly demonstrate the school's intentions for children's learning and be a way of increasing the likelihood of achieving the targets shared by children, parents and teachers. It is the school's chance to say to those who pay for it, those whose children use it and the community at large which has great expectations of the school,

 *This is what we believe; This is what we intend to do; This is how we will assess your children's progress whilst they are with us.*

This is your opportunity to make clear that we are about pupils increasing their knowledge and understanding whilst they are in school.

The process of the policy's development may:
- help participants understand teaching, learning and assessment strategies employed by other staff;
- help create a team spirit in making public the school's goals;
- offer a means of evaluation of the work being planned;
- help clarify functions and responsibilities of staff; and
- help new staff to settle in.

A well-defined and readable document should give useful information to parents, governors and inspectors. What do parents really want to know? Many parents will be content with a general outline of the assessment routines and the frequency with which they will be used whist their children are moving through the school. Some may in addition wish to know the Programmes of Study that you will be using in order that they can better help their children at home. But mostly parents will want to know that they will be kept closely informed about how their child is doing in comparison with others in his/her class, in the school, in the locality and nationally. A whole-school policy will make it clear to any parents what information they will have and when. As we discuss later, governors too will want to know factual information and the way in which resource allocation is spent and how this relates to achievement. Governors can be instrumental in setting up the policy (Chapter 2) and join target setting groups (Chapter 5). They may also be interested in the evaluations you make about the effectiveness of your spending decisions. Inspectors are dealt with in Chapter 8, but suffice to say here that as well as the information above they would expect to see in your policy some detail about the way in which the policy is monitored and any recent changes made in areas in the light of experience.

The document should provide a useful framework for individual teacher's planning and this is covered in Chapter 3. The test of a good policy document is how frequently it is referred to in the course of planning a lesson, sequence of lessons or in medium-term planning. Is your school's document left in the drawer and only brought out on high days, holidays and OFSTED days? Considering the effort which is invested in these few sheets of paper, surely it should be the focus of attention for some of the time? When completed your document should aid coherence, continuity, progression and shape priorities amongst staff. It should help teachers to speak to each other about their work, and help them to understand how their own contribution fits in with the efforts of others.

The end result should assist in achieving uniformity and consistency in school decision making by helping to focus the minds of various decision making groups, such as governors, the senior management team, and your fellow subject coordinators, toward common aims.

A host of factors can help or hinder the development of assessment practices in any school. The attitude of the head, influential governors, the way any excess money is allocated and when necessary where the cuts should fall. Having an agreed policy document which has been discussed by staff and governors and shown to parents can then help to influence key decision making groups towards your aims and objectives, or at least make them feel they will have a fight on their hands if they choose to weald the axe in your direction.

The process in which you will engage may help colleagues to understand teaching and learning strategies employed by other staff. A democratic forum where best practice is also rehearsed and the discussion on the ways in which teachers are successful in various parts of the school should not only provide you with a better policy but also help teachers to learn from one another. Indeed your work in this area might have contributed to the creation of a greater team spirit in making public the school's goals and providing a forum whereby teachers can act as a professional critical friend.

As coordinator, you will be the key person in developing a whole-school approach to assessment. You will need to ensure the commitment of all staff which Mortimer's team (mentioned earlier) showed to be vital to the success of any significant initiative. Thus it is not enough to go to a staff meeting and agree that you will conjure up and present an assessment policy even though in many schools the English, mathematics and science coordinators would be quite content for you to do all the work. What would then happen in practice is that your policy would be presented to the staff for discussion and perhaps minor changes suggested. Everybody would have had involvement in the policy process but would not be committed to it. It will just be left to the assessment coordinator and the policy will disappear into folders, never again to see the light of day.

The difference between involvement and commitment is best summed up in the tale of the American breakfast — fried eggs and bacon. To produce such a meal the chicken was of course involved. However, the pig was fully committed!

Assessment coordinators need to emphasise Mortimer's point about greater progress being made by children when there is a limited focus of activities in the classroom at any one time. This applies equally to assessment practices. Trying to assess too much, or indeed too many children, will lead to dilution of the quality (and hence usefulness) of the results.

The assessment coordinator needs to take the lead. You may even write the policy at home but all staff need to have the opportunity not merely to comment on the policy document but also to trial activities. All staff need to write drafts for their own age-range; to look at and comment on good and bad examples of records etc. otherwise consistency will be lost.

The creation of a mission statement can be the initiative that binds staff together and many headteachers have drawn on the values within such a statement to help define the other policies created in order to help the school cope with the demands placed upon it. The mission statement itself is supposed to sum up the reason for the school's existence, its chief priorities. The obvious analogy is the moonshot. The mission of Apollo 10 was to land a man on the moon. All the technical, staff, financial and training considerations were to this end. The mission defined the amount of money needed, the specification of the vehicle, the training the astronauts would need. Schools are not, however, one-shot enterprises and so this is where frequently the analogy falls down. Schools run on an externally determined budget and exist variously to socialise their pupils into the ways of society; to get children to appreciate beauty; to turn them into Christians; to allow them to demonstrate sporting prowess; to learn the three Rs.

The process of determining your mission, or statement of intent, will bring differences in priorities into focus and allow staff to gain some agreement between themselves as to what the joint enterprise is for.

The mission statement could read:

The mission of the governors and staff of Swan Primary School, in conjunction with parents, is to create an intellectual, physical and social environment for the education of the 'whole child' characterised by:
- a continual drive to improve standards so that every child maximises learning and achievement;
- ensuring that each child makes the transition from Key Stage 1 to Key Stage 2 to Key Stage 3 smoothly and with as little anxiety as possible;

- instilling children with expectations about their capacity to learn and achieve success through effort;
- providing children with opportunities to celebrate their own achievements with humility and be generous in the celebration of the achievements of others;
- the development and mastery by pupils of the broadest possible range of skills — thinking, oracy, numeracy, literacy, communication, listening and dexterity; and
- providing all children with full access to the whole curriculum regardless of their sex, culture or any disability.

Covey uses well the tale of the large American battleship sailing at night during the last war. The man on deck sees a bright light in front of him and send out a radio message saying 'My name is Able Seaman Smith — we are a very large battleship and are steering at 24 knots — would you move?' The message comes back 'My name is Able Seaman Jones — you move'. The seaman then calls up his lieutenant who says 'My name's Lieutenant Roberts — I'm in charge at the helm of the largest battleship known to man and its sailing your way — would you give, way, please?' The message came back 'My name's Able Seaman Jones — you give way!'. So then they wake the Admiral and the Admiral says 'I'm Admiral Jackson and I'm in charge of the largest battleship known to man and steaming at 25 knots in your direction, can you please move **now**'. Finally the message came back 'My name's Able Seaman Jones — we are a lighthouse!'. The Admiral ordered the helmsman to alter course.

Even if we have an unassailable case with ultimate authority we all need to know what lies in front of us.

A mission statement such as this therefore defines the assessment policy in terms of the school's purpose. Once the mission statement is agreed and understood then you can start as an assessment coordinator looking at the way to establish the policy to support the mission.

You will need to use tactics. What do you want the policy to say? How will this be achieved? What will you be content with? And when you have decided this, how will you paint the picture for the staff? Creating a vision is no easy matter. What seems obvious to you may not have occurred to many of those you will need to influence. Stephen Covey (1992) in his book *Seven Habits of Highly Effective People* has a lesson for assessment coordinators to show that they need to know the way and work out a route for their journey. You wouldn't after all go on a long journey without knowing the destination. We all need to know what's in front of us. You need to know how you're going to handle difficult staff (see Thomas, 1998). You need to know where the money will come from to finance this activity and what INSET will be needed.

Setting a framework for change will be simpler if you use the principles set out in this book. Your first tactics should be to weave assessment into the your school's development plan. Work out the costs. How much are the NFER tests going to cost on a yearly basis, or the setting up of Records of Achievement (RoA)? Try at all times to be proactive. Don't just let things happen.

In all of this the assessment coordinator needs to be seen as a role model. You need to be seen as the expert. You may not feel that you are very expert but people will assume you to be, especially if you can go on the right development courses and if you read this book carefully and adopt some of its ideas.

## The role of the assessment coordinator

In his influential work *Management Teams: Why They Succeed or Fail*, Meredith Belbin (1981) shows that a successful team needs people with skills, knowledge, aptitudes, interests and personalities which interlock in order to make a workable organisation. There is also a need for leadership to create a shared sense of purpose, giving direction to the team. These leadership functions in primary schools have increasingly been shared with classteachers through the policy of curriculum coordination. In 1978 the DES survey *Primary Education in England* showed the many ways in which posts of responsibility were starting to be used in primary schools to improve the consistency of work in a number of subject areas, but particularly in language and mathematics.

There then followed a growing recognition of the value of headteachers delegating curriculum responsibility in all subjects and some aspects such as home-school links, early years and assessment. Consultants, implying specialist expertise, have become coordinators, suggesting a managerial role.

Mike Harrison and Steve Gill (1992), in their book *Primary School Management*, argue that the degree to which any particular primary school has developed such policies may be indicated by:

- the nature of the decisions coordinators feel confident in making without recourse to the head;
- the understanding of the role shown by the person or persons to whom each coordinator is responsible and the mechanisms by which their work is monitored;
- the degree of consideration of personal needs and circumstances demonstrated in the choice and handling of coordinators;

The School Management Task Force (DES, 1991) opens its report by stating:

 *Successful schools do not simply happen: they are successful because people make them so and all such people have a stake in management.*

- the strength of the structures of organisation which support coordinators (e.g. class release time, training);
- whether coordinators are respected as models of good practice in their specialist areas;
- does the headteacher act as a good working model for the relationships coordinators are encouraged to develop with other teachers?
- the ways in which coordinators are enabled to learn personnel management skills from each other; and
- the degree to which coordinators work in harmony with the school's stated aims.

In primary schools, responsibility for the work of each individual class is effectively devolved to their classteacher. Many headteachers appear to be increasingly displaced from teaching, learning and curricular issues (Blease and Lever, 1992). Whether this state of affairs leads to independence or interdependence will depend on both the school's management structure, the level of active management and the skills of the school's curriculum coordinators.

For the assessment coordinator to be effective all the staff need to have a clear understanding about the role he or she is expected to play within a team of professionals. In *The Developing School* Peter Holly and Geoff Southworth (1989) discuss several whole-school concerns which impinge on the effectiveness of coordinators.

For instance they claim that groups of teachers who are more receptive to a collaborative approach grow to respect and acknowledge curriculum expertise from within their own ranks. With such an ethos it is more likely that agreement can be reached about where classroom autonomy ends and responsibility towards a whole-school policy begins. This is an issue which, quite rightly, will vary widely from school to school, but will inevitably lead to trouble if it varies from class to class within one school. The value placed on reviews and evaluations of aspects of a teacher's work being done by peers, rather than the headteacher, is highly significant. It will also be an important indicator of the school's readiness for devolved responsibility. A collaborative atmosphere can be maintained only where changes introduced are consistently seen to benefit children throughout the school rather than merely to advantage the reputation of the initiator.

In schools where job descriptions are highly prescriptive, there is little room for individual enterprise and initiative. Job specifications need to show that the school has different expectations of a newly appointed coordinator than from one who has been in post for some time. The willingness of teachers to accept advice depends on their perception of the assessment coordinator's ability in the classroom. Teachers will also make judgments as to the value of the advice based on your range of experience, ability to organise resources, knowledge of the subject and range of interpersonal skills. You need to make sure that these are presented to colleagues in the best possible light.

As you become more confident in your middle-management role, arguing changes and making principled educational judgments, headteachers must accept that their own views will be challenged more frequently. Headteachers who see this as rivalry to their professional authority rather than as an intellectual challenge will be likely to undermine the confidence of coordinators and hinder them from accepting greater managerial involvement. However, you may consider it wise to be circumspect at first in expressing too many opinions at variance with the head! Managerial responsibility and support for the coordination of the coordinators must be made explicit. Who is to monitor your work as a manager of assessment practices and offer guidance at critical times?

School time needs to be budgeted with the creation of effective coordination policies as a priority. Time available for assessment coordinators to do the paperwork will affect the degree of consultation possible and hence its quality. Time for assessment coordinators to work alongside teachers in their classrooms will be necessary in order to change practice. Time to allow you to see teaching and learning in parts of the school with which you are unfamiliar will be required for your own development.

Measures need to be taken to overcome role ambivalence. Primary coordinators have in the past often proved reluctant to direct colleagues and enforce ideas. Many teachers see their coordinating role as restricted to writing paper policies and offering tips. Traditionally, primary teachers do not offer comment on colleagues' teaching styles, approach and lesson plans, or act as critical friends, which would be necessary if the twelve principles described in the last chapter are to become a reality. Coordinators also do not frequently report colleagues for not following the school's policy. Those teachers selected as coordinators need to be helped through training to behave more assertively. Whole-school commitment to improving standards of teaching performance would help acceptance.

The speed with which changes can be brought about may depend on the availability of appropriate INSET. The school has to actively promote acceptance that the nature of this devolved responsibility implies emphasis upon managerial skill as well as upon curriculum expertise. Thus teachers selected to become coordinators will need to develop skills in areas such as the implementation of change, curriculum planning, evaluation and school development, in addition to attending subject based courses. There is also a need to help coordinators develop interpersonal skills.

Success is likely to be greater where headteachers and the senior management team actively support the work of their coordinators. This may involve showing respect for local knowledge, giving additional resources when needed and managing information to this end. Coordinators who are asked for regular reports on their work are more likely to feel that what they are doing is important.

## A personal strategy for assessment coordinators

 *No matter how committed you are to the importance of assessment, and no matter how expert you are in ways of doing it and knowing the technical terms to use, it will be all to no avail if you cannot be a good manager.*

(David and Wendy Clemson, 1996)

As we have argued above, the circumstances in which assessment coordinators find themselves will affect the way in which they can carry out their work and influence others. If you are the coordinator, whether your school situation is ideal or not, by considering your actions carefully you can determine the most appropriate way to ensure progress. In *Primary School Management* (1992) Mike Harrison and Steve Gill discuss ways that both newly appointed coordinators and those who have been in post for some time might fulfil their roles:

**Arrange to go into other teachers' classrooms to work with them, if possible**

You will need to consider the reasons you give teachers for your presence. Are you to be there as a critical friend; to give an example of good practice in your subject; to focus on an area the teacher has identified; to discover the quality of the teacher's work in your area or to give advice?

To whom should you report what you find in other teachers' classrooms? Is this information for your headteacher, deputy, the governors, senior management team or for the classteacher only? Is the decision yours?

**Try to develop the necessary interpersonal skills to carry out your coordination roles successfully**

Do you have any responsibility to help others to gain these skills? Can you learn from the mistakes and skills of others? Can you help others learn? Are you able to take advantage of management courses as well as those for your particular curriculum area?

**Understand the scope of your responsibilities and where they fit into the management structure of the school**

You will be carrying out a delegated responsibility on behalf of the headteacher. Can you establish with him or her agreed terms of reference? Where is the dividing line between a classteacher's autonomy and your responsibility? Can you persuade your headteacher to play an active role in defining these boundaries? Make sure that you recognise the school's stated central purpose and aims in the work you do and the changes you are trying to effect. Refer to the school's mission statement.

(after Harrison and Gill, *Primary School Management*, 1992, p. 37)

## Making change happen

The task is not impossible. Most teachers do want to improve their practice. That is, they want to see the children in their care develop and to teach as effectively as possible.

 *Over the last ten years and certainly since the introduction of the National Curriculum, teachers have made many changes. Unfortunately, this has led to some reinforcement of the idea that making change is always personally stressful, that it regularly leads to a blind alley and that it always results in an increased workload.*                    (Harrison and Cross, 1993)

Change can have compensations. For example Anne Edwards (1993) argues that a policy of using teacher coordinators as change agents in their areas of expertise would allow us to preserve those things which represent the best in primary education, such as the classteacher system, the family atmosphere and close contact with parents, whilst at the same time adopting whole-school curriculum development and effective in-house INSET.

Change is an interesting area of human experience as attitudes to it tend to be self-perpetuating. It is almost always the case that the individual who dislikes change will have difficulty with that change and will rarely be totally positive about its results. The attitude of the participants seems to be the most influential factor in its successful implementation. Coordinators therefore need to persuade, cajole and affect the attitudes of staff toward:
1   The need for change
2   The focus of the change (adoption of the 12 principles)
3   The change process itself

Change is never achieved solely as the result of a management plan, government legislation or incidental INSET. In *Making School-centred INSET Work*, Patrick Easen (1989) comments:

 *One difficulty about in-service programmes ... concerns who is defining the needs for whom. There is a conventional*

> *wisdom which sees in-service work as being designed by 'task analysis' and 'needs assessment'. In other words, the task to be accomplished is analysed in terms of specific behaviours to be acquired.*

This wins no one to their cause. Change only occurs when teachers believe in the need for it, know where it is going, are committed to it and have some ownership of it.

As assessment coordinator your first considerations must be:
- How much do you know about the past and present situation and the opinions of the teachers with whom you will be working?
- How clear are you about the change you require?
- What will you be satisfied with?
- Are you willing to be fully committed to and involved with colleagues?
- Are you prepared to make the change?

Thus key personal skills which coordinators will need to develop in order to promote classroom change include:
- to act consistently;
- to maintain hope, belief and optimism;
- to want success (although not necessarily public approval);
- to be willing to take calculated risks and accept the consequences;
- to develop a capacity to accept, deal with and use conflict constructively;
- to learn to use a soft voice and low key manner;
- to develop self awareness;
- to cultivate a tolerance of ambiguity and complexity;
- to avoid viewing issues as simply black and white;
- to become an active listener.

(adapted from Everard and Morris, 1985, p. 181)

The change process may develop its own momentum and may keep itself going, although it is more likely to require continual re-emphasis. Assessment coordinators must accept that teachers' initial enthusiasm may be short-lived when they discover the full implications of the change. This book attempts to guide you through the process.

| | |
|---|---|
| **Assess the current situation in your school** | You will need to be open about what you are doing and to beware of raising the profile of this curriculum area by too much too soon. We all react to having issues forced upon us! Look listen and learn. |
| **Gather information** | Find out the quality and extent of current assessment. Identify where teachers show assessment on their curriculum planning forecasts. (Chapter 3) |
| **Find evidence** | Examine school documentation. Is assessment referred to consistently? |
| **Ask questions** | Listen if colleagues talk about assessment issues. Find out whether there have been previous initiatives. How have colleagues responded to change in the past? |
| **Consider outside influences** | Make sure that you have read advice from the QCA, OFSTED, TTA or DfEE. Make contact with the local adviser with responsibility for assessment, or a university where advice may be available. Take note of any courses which might help you or your colleagues. |
| **Build the need** | Establish a file where you keep your notes, relevant documents and a diary. |
| **Talk to the headteacher in order to** | Discover the head's thoughts and commitment to assessment; determine its current priority within the school development plan; establish a professional dialogue between you and the headteacher; register your interest and commitment; negotiate the next step; emphasise the need; formulate a rationale and targets. |
| **Construct a plan of action** | Who can help us? How can we help ourselves? How will we know when we get there? |
| **Write a statement of intent with colleagues** | This will remind you of your distant aims even when absorbed by little local difficulties. The process of writing itself can act as a catalyst. (This chapter) |
| **Invite outsiders in** | Outsiders can have a range of effects. They can present new ideas, absorb colleagues' hostility, say things you might not dare to say and clearly state the need as well as provide a more objective view. Unfortunately, they may also steer teachers in an unpredicted direction, stir up a hornets' nest and worse, not be credible to your teachers. (Chapter 6) |
| **Visit a local school** | This might be a visit for you, you and your head or the whole staff. Avoid authority show-schools but choose one where the corresponding coordinator is like minded and where they face challenges of a similar order. |
| **Use ghosts** | A 'ghost' is a person, body or event outside the school, the requirements of which may be cited as a need to make a particular change (the government, the LEA, a local initiative). Beware of over-playing this strategy. So many people use it, teachers are good at side stepping this one! |
| **Run a series of staff meetings and/or a professional development day** | It is likely that such meetings will be the core of any discussion that your teachers are involved in, particularly in the early stages. They must be planned with care, one successful one is far better than a series which lead nowhere. (This chapter) |
| **Build from existing strengths** | Find out what individual strengths in assessment there are amongst the staff. This is where we ask classteachers to start from. It is not unreasonable that we should display this good practice in a management situation. |
| **Tackle classroom management issues early on** | There are few issues to do with primary schooling which do not impinge on classroom management. It is the matter which leads most frequently to the failure of change in the classroom. Avoid descriptions which emphasise polarities, such as — structured or unstructured, didactic or discovery methods, child led or teacher led. No-one has the right to be an island because children pass from one class to another. Hence consistency and continuity demand some common practice. |
| **Use children and their learning as a constant reference point** | All teachers have children's learning as a common goal, so use it. Ask colleagues how their children might react to an activity. If you know the children it may be useful to refer to individuals. Ask colleagues about the range of abilities in their group. Encourage teachers to bring children's work along to meetings. (Chapter 8) |
| **Use literacy and numeracy as common reference points** | These aspects of the curriculum are common to all age groups and teachers have a real desire to develop them. Assessment in these areas is central to current concerns so use this focus to help you. (Chapter 3) |

| Provide advice as coordinator | It may not be possible for you personally to answer everyone's questions but it is important that answers are found. You may be able to refer to resources or to other people or places where the issue can be addressed. A network of information, contacts, friends, and references will be invaluable to you. |
|---|---|
| Provide a resource base | This is something that you can develop from day one. You may have little in the way of funds but invariably you can make a start by establishing a resource for teachers. Putting together materials for developing teachers' subject knowledge might be a good start. Why not make available the TTA CD ROM 'assessing your needs' which has film action and sound? Establishing a resource centre will have several effects. It will help to establish that you are the coordinator, that the job needs doing and that doing the job has direct benefits to your teacher colleagues. |
| Set attainable goals | Small steps, like asking teachers to assess a small group, may lead through success to larger strides. Teachers who experience perceived failure are sometimes very hard to re-motivate. |
| Become a professional friend | Strong personal relationships with colleagues may help or hinder your initiatives. Friendly or not, however, you must strive for a professional relationship. This means you can trust one another with teaching and learning as the focus of relationships. In order to build such a relationship you may have to demonstrate your skills and admit to one or two personal weaknesses. |
| Avoid bottomless pits | Some colleagues will absorb all of your energy and give nothing in return. You have limited time and cannot afford to devote it to lost causes. These teachers may well have to be worked around. This is not an excuse however to ignore those teachers who might well have doubts, those who feel insecure with the changes you are instigating and who are not immediate converts. These teachers are your challenge, the reason you have the post you hold. It is by the changes in **their** behaviour you will be able to measure your progress. |
| Act like a swan | Even in the most difficult of times swans appear calm and tranquil on the surface even if actually paddling like fury underneath. |
| Evaluate what you have done | Evaluation has to be an ongoing process, rather than something which we do later to determine our level of success. Evaluation needs to be inherent in the process rather than merely a step in the management plan. Periodic reviews where we assess, evaluate, refocus and re-emphasise are part of that process but not the whole story. Be sure to act on the result of the evaluation. Teachers will value the process if it leads to something but are naturally wary of anything which seems like time wasting. It is essential that both you and your colleagues are clear about your aims.' In order to evaluate, we must first know what we mean by **value**. What positive outcomes did we seek to achieve?' (Novak and Gowin, 1984) |

# Skills for successful coordination

In addition to whole-school pre-requisites, personal skills and attitudes will, of course, greatly influence the achievements of the coordinator. Management at all levels is predominantly about interpersonal relationships. Thus curriculum coordinators need to consider the range of their interpersonal skills and how to get their messages across.

## Effective communication

Some teachers may find that their opportunities to influence colleagues is limited. The method they use to get their message across may be as important as the content itself.

It may help to establish some guidelines for effective communication. The following list is based on the principles in Joan Dean's (1987) book *Managing the Primary School*.

- Teachers are more likely to be responsive to the advice of coordinators if addressed personally rather than anonymously in a staff meeting or by memo.
- Coordinators will need to learn that with teachers, just as with children, rousing the interest of the listener is necessary in order to get your message across.
- Information is more likely to be valued if it gives an advantage in power or status to the listener.
- No-one likes to be seen as letting down their team or working group. It is desirable sometimes for coordinators to present their information in such a way that it requires action upon which others will rely.
- Teachers charged with the responsibility of promoting curricular areas to their colleagues may find an advantage in choosing an appropriate messenger. The status of the source of the information is often seen to indicate its importance.
- The situation (surroundings, time of day etc.) should be chosen carefully in order to predispose the listener to be receptive.

## Making meetings effective

Meetings are the most common method that coordinators use in an attempt to get their message over, but they are not always a success. Just having a meeting is not enough. The prime consideration must be: *What do you want to happen at the meeting?* This point is seldom addressed, for many meetings need never happen at all. Harrison (1995) claims you may need to call a meeting:

**To communicate information**
Assessment coordinators will need to give information to their colleagues. Often this information can be given out in written form with only a brief explanation needed, possibly without having a meeting at all. The skill you will need to develop is to ensure that the information is read and acted upon. Wasting every one's time for an hour, to compensate for your lack of foresight in not preparing a briefing sheet however, does not go down well with busy teachers.

**To generate discussion**

If you want teachers to discuss issues, they need to have been properly prepared beforehand by being given the relevant information. You may need to arrange the seating in such a way that everyone can see each other in order to encourage participation. A brainstorming session recorded on tape can generate ideas or possible solutions.

The key to success for this type of meeting is to create an atmosphere which encourages staff to share ideas and perceptions. They will not do this if early statements (however much at odds with your wishes) are not accepted, at least as starting points for the generation of further ideas.

**To make corporate decisions**

If coordinators are organising a meeting to reach a decision on a key topic it is vital that everyone is made aware that the meeting has this purpose. Time has to be allowed beforehand, such that small group meetings can already have aired some of the issues. Make sure teachers have had time to read and absorb printed material. Decide before the meeting if you intend to take a vote if necessary, or whether it would be more appropriate to continue the debate until a consensus is reached.

Coordinators will be more effective if they understand the difference between the various purposes of these staff meetings and realise what can go wrong. We have all attended meetings which were monopolised by one person, had too many important items left to the end, or failed to get people involved. Occasionally all these things happen in the one meeting. We have also all attended well-run friendly and relaxed meetings which kept to the point and seemed like time well spent.

Coordinators need to consider a variety of strategies for organising and chairing meetings. Their aim should be to ensure that as many as possible of the negative features are avoided and the positive ones achieved. Playfoot, Skelton and Southworth (1989) give further useful information on the conduct of effective meetings in school.

The role of the assessment coordinator is pretty similar to that of the role of any other curriculum subject leader. The TTA (1998) define four key areas of subject leadership:

| Subject leaders should have knowledge and understanding of: | All my subject leader colleagues | Some of my subject leader colleagues | Hardly any subject leader colleagues |
|---|---|---|---|
| any statutory curriculum requirements for the subject and the requirements for assessment, recording and reporting of pupils' attainment and progress; | | | |
| how evidence from relevant research and inspection evidence and local national and international standards of achievement in the subject can be used to inform expectations, targets and teaching approaches; | | | |
| how to use comparative data, together with information about pupils' prior attainment, to establish benchmarks and set targets for improvement. | | | |
| **Subject leaders should be able to develop and implement subject policies, plans, targets and practices. They:** | | | |
| use data effectively to identify pupils who are underachieving in the subject and, where necessary, create and implement effective plans of action to support those pupils; | | | |
| analyse and interpret relevant national, local and school data, plus research and inspection evidence, to inform policies, practices, expectations, targets and teaching methods; | | | |
| establish, with the involvement of relevant staff, short, medium and long term plans for the development and resourcing of the subject which are based on a range of comparative information and evidence, including in relation to the attainment of pupils; | | | |
| identify realistic and challenging targets for improvement in the subject. | | | |
| **Subject leaders secure and sustain effective teaching of the subject, evaluate the quality of teaching and standards of pupils' achievements and set targets for improvement. They:** | | | |
| establish and implement clear policies and practices for assessing, recording and reporting on pupil achievement, and for using this information to recognise achievement and to assist pupils in setting targets for further improvement; | | | |
| ensure that information about pupils' achievements in previous classes and schools is used effectively to secure good progress in the subject; | | | |
| establish a partnership with parents to involve them in their child's learning of the subject, as well as providing information about curriculum, assessment, progress and targets. | | | |

Source: TTA (1998a)

Finally, your headteacher has an important role to play. The TTA standards for headteachers state (TTA, 1998c) that headteachers should have a knowledge and understanding of:

- strategies to achieve effective teaching and learning of literacy and numeracy;
- how to use comparative data, together with information about pupils' prior attainment, to establish benchmarks and set targets for improvement;
- requirements and models for the curriculum and its assessment; and
- effective teaching and assessment methods, including the use of information and communications technology.

If some teachers have some way to go then, using such an audit, you will need to develop a plan to familiarise your teachers with each of the competences. This book will help you to do so but bear in mind that 'when change is agreed, it is those who are best at doing things the old way who have the most to lose, but by the same token they have the most to offer too' (Tagg, 1996).

# Chapter 3    Planning for assessment

> *Planning is an unnatural activity. It is far more fun to **do** something. The nicest thing about **not** planning is that failure comes as a complete surprise rather than being preceded by a period of worry and depression.*
>                                  (John Harvey-Jones)

Your colleagues may not be so aware of the necessity to establish the important link between planning and assessment as you are. The interdependence of planning and assessment, firmly established in the Dearing Report, has now been accepted as a key element in the development of a policy to ensure quality assessment in primary schools. You may need to use a number of arguments to get your staff to appreciate this fact for 'Failure to plan is planning for failure' (John Harvey-Jones).

The failure of many schools to have systematic planning processes and the consequent criticism by OFSTED has persuaded some.

> *There's an increasing recognition of the need for better curriculum planning to support pupils within mixed ability classes and working to their full potential.*
>                                  (OFSTED, 1994a, p. 22)

SCAA (1995) informed schools that:

> *schools should consider their policy on assessment to ensure that it provides a manageable framework for promoting accurate*

Mere chance must not be the arbiter of educational provision. Through our planning we can try to achieve some control over the future. Planning is about anticipation, forethought and action, not reaction. But in order to plan, it is necessary to look at experience as well as prescience. In assessment terms there are two essential aspects of good planning that we would like to find in more common use in our primary schools: the systematic use of experiential data, and the overt forging of connections between curriculum (as taught) and curriculum (as assessed).                    (Clemson and Clemson, 1996)

*and consistent assessment across the curriculum. Assessment is an integral part of teaching and learning and the time allocation at the long-term level of planning will need to reflect this. The assessment policy will also inform subsequent medium- and short-term planning by clarifying the school's approaches to:*

- *the identification of clear learning objectives;*
- *how and when children's progress will be assessed and*
- *the use of assessment to match work to the learning needs of children.*          (Planning the Curriculum at Key Stages 1 and 2)

Planning will also need to take account of the time required to carry out statutory tests and tasks at the end of each key stage.

It can be seen that the establishment of clear learning objectives lies at the heart of good quality teacher assessment *and* planning. Accurate and appropriate assessment results will not be obtained without the teacher being primed to uncover elements of pupils' thinking and performance unless this is planned into the lesson, and the children stand little chance of giving their best unless the planning for teaching is good.

However, planning is another word which sometimes makes teachers' hearts sink. Some systems they have been forced to follow are over-bureaucratic to the extent that they place an unnecessary burden on teachers. Some teachers have been subject to planning processes that consist of merely responding to page upon page of headings without being given any signs that the system contributes to better teaching or to a rise in the standards achieved by children. Frequently these systems do not provide individual teachers with a framework that is both useful and manageable. Some teachers have shown us planning files which provide them with no support. One is tempted to say that some headteachers are asking for information which indeed distracts teachers from the real business of preparing to teach. There is frequently little evidence of the sharing of good practice, no sharp assessment of learning, nothing informing future teaching.

It is essential to have a systematic planning structure in place so that all staff know what has to be recorded. The three layers of planning (long-, medium- and short-term) need to be the same format for all teachers in the school in order for it to be effective.

Curriculum planning is carried out differently by individuals and various groups of teachers. It is also carried out differently in individual schools but it is possible to identify three broad levels of planning.

These are:

**Long-term planning**
> This is concerned with producing a framework for each year of Key Stage 1 and Key Stage 2. It should reflect the school's policy and everybody in the school ranging from governors to staff needs to be involved in the creation of such plans.

**Medium-term planning**
> This deals with the subject programmes of work to be taught to each year group. It also provides an excellent opportunity for teachers to identify key areas of assessment. It could involve year group or Key Stage 1 / 2 teachers supported by senior management.

**Short-term planning**
> This is usually carried out individually by class teachers and is used to schedule the day to day teaching and assessment of children. The short-term plan can then be broken down into weekly and daily planning which will be discussed later in this chapter.

## Long-term planning

If you ask your colleagues about any problems they might have in planning the curriculum they may produce a list that includes lack of experience and training, resources, ineffective leadership, but most of them would certainly list the problem of time. However long the list, the most important of these is always identified as time. Good use of the time available and the structure of the learning objectives around this number of lessons, this available time, is the key to *Planning the Curriculum at Key Stages 1 and 2* (SCAA, 1995). This publication highlights the key areas in long-term planning.

SCAA recognised that no two schools are the same and so proposed that a number of factors which would vary from school to school needed to be included:

- The school's aims, objectives and policies
- The revised subject orders — religious education and other curriculum provision determined by the school
- A realistic assessment of time available for teaching
- The school's approach to managing the curriculum
- Staff experience and expertise
- Subject knowledge and familiarity with the revised subject orders
- How children learn the characteristics of the key stages
- The needs, abilities, interests and achievements of the child
- The school's resources and accommodation
- The teaching opportunities provided by the locality

(SCAA, 1995, p. 27)

There are a number of additional considerations to take into account, for instance,

- schools not exempted by their local SACRE, need to make time for daily worship;
- all schools need to undertake regular programmes of educational visits for pupils to gain first hand experiences;
- the need for primary schools to be able to change lessons because of day to day events;
- the DfEE recommendations for the length of the school weeks as 21 hours at Key Stage 1 and 23.5 hours at Key Stage 2.
- an understanding amongst staff that good quality planning is a necessary pre-requisite to good quality assessment.

Those coordinators who find themselves involved in this process, or even in charge of it, may be interested in the following case study.

## A case study

The school on which this study is modelled used a set of staged meetings to begin the process. The management team recognised that each stage needed the agreement of the whole school for it to succeed just as staff-wide involvement is needed to raise standards. The stages were as follows:

**Stage 1** The management team gained whole-staff agreement to adopt the minimum teaching week as recommended by the DfEE. The staff also grew to recognise that this is active teaching and learning time — as opposed to say: waiting for the midday staff; biscuit and milk time; excessive time spent changing for PE and time spent on nothing in particular between registration and assembly. This was a pre-requisite for the rest of the process.

**Stage 2** They began a discussion to agree the basis for the division of the available curriculum time amongst different aspects of the curriculum. (756 hours at Key Stage 1 and 846 hours at Key Stage 2 over the course of a 36 week year). Problems were then ironed out, for example, it was found that instead of doing 846 hours they currently only did 840 hrs of active teaching in Key Stage 2. However, it didn't take long to realise that to find six hours over the course of the year was not very difficult. The school cut assemblies down by a couple of minutes a day which 'found' the six hours easily.

**Stage 3** The staff had agreed that we would decrease by 20 per cent the 'Dearing bonus' (the time we have outside the statutory National Curriculum) and use 5 per cent of this for physical education. The reason for this was that swimming was so time-consuming. However, this was the start of some disagreement.

**Stage 4** The whole staff had agreed to adopt the recommendation of the distribution of hours between the subjects from the Dearing Report (section 4.20 on subject distribution). This marked an important development because for the first time teachers were going to plan under subject headings. With the introduction of the National Numeracy and Literacy Strategies that time-per-subject accounting seems to have become the accepted format. We look forward to the next instalment — probably the science half hour and the ICT 5 minutes!

**Stage 5** The staff decided to divide the 36 week accounting year into three thus to plan each term over the course of only twelve weeks. This was a most sensible move because it meant that the school had recognised that other things happen in schools around Christmas and sports days, visits and the coming to school of various theatre groups, also are an entitlement for primary school pupils. That is what gives this phase its character. Therefore they planned for the curriculum to be covered in twelve weeks each term which gave teachers the time to undertake all the activities that go on in primary schools, without sacrificing the planned lesson sequence. This system will become more familiar to schools as the numeracy project initiative becomes more widespread. This project also uses 12 week planning periods.

**Stage 6** The staff agreed on the following subject frequency. Each term they taught English, maths, science, art, music, PE and RE and in two terms per year decided to teach history, geography and technology. All of this was in accordance with SCAA recommendations. The above framework took a number of staff meetings to evolve and laid the foundations for the following summary chart.

|                       | Eng | Maths | Science | Technology | History | Geography | Art | Music | PE | RE |
|-----------------------|-----|-------|---------|------------|---------|-----------|-----|-------|----|----|
| Key Stage 1 % hours   | 24  | 17    | 7       | 5          | 5       | 5         | 5   | 5     | 5  | 5  |
| Key Stage 2 % hours   | 19  | 15    | 8.5     | 5          | 5       | 5         | 5   | 5     | 5  | 5  |

Using these percentages yielded the following subject hours (divide by three for termly totals).

|                     | Eng | Maths | Science | Technology | History | Geography | Art | Music | PE | RE |
|---------------------|-----|-------|---------|------------|---------|-----------|-----|-------|----|----|
| Hours in Key Stage 2 | 162 | 126   | 75      | 45         | 45      | 45        | 45  | 45    | 90 | 45 |

From the autumn term 1999, all primary and special schools should teach a daily mathematics lesson to all pupils, lasting between 45 and 60 minutes depending on pupils' ages. Teachers should teach the whole class together for a high proportion of the lesson, and oral and mental work should feature strongly in each lesson.

(*Final Report of the National Numeracy Project, NNP, 1998*)

PE had to be increased because of the swimming problem already mentioned — Swimming is still mandatory in all primary schools. Even so, the science coordinator didn't like the idea that PE was getting more time than her core subject. However, the idea of using time as the determinant for long-term planning was the central planning concept adopted by the staff. It solved problems such as how to fit in all one would like to do about 'the Victorians' — a typical primary topic. History has to be confined to 45 hours. Hence in a 36 week year this gives only just over an hour a week. You simply cannot teach the whole of the content of the Victorians and have therefore to be much sharper about the content and define exactly what your learning objectives should be. Teachers simply haven't got the time, the hours, to do anything else.

With the introduction of the numeracy and literacy hours, the utilisation of the basic hours per year will need to alter for those schools which choose to follow it. The additional time will have to be found by slimming down other subjects. QCA (1998) has made some suggestions as to how this might be done:

- **prioritising** on the core subjects and using teachers' professional judgment to decide which aspects of the foundation subjects to concentrate on;
- **combining** National Curriculum subjects, particularly where attainment objectives are closely allied;
- **reducing** the scope of the work to be covered within each of the subjects.

If a good quality long-term plan exists, then there is an excellent basis for planning assessment foci in the medium- and short-term.

## Medium-term planning

This phase in the planning cycle provides the necessary link between the long (*one word description*) and short (*this is what my lesson will look like*) term. The main learning objectives are identified from the National Curriculum and provide a focus for teaching and assessment. At this stage the resources, human and physical, desired parental involvement, and links between subjects need to be identified.

As in Figure 3.1 the identification of the learning objectives for the unit of study give teachers a vehicle not only to teach, but also to assess learning, thus building to a 'best fit' level description. It can be argued that it is the clarity with which such planned learning outcomes can be identified which is the differentiator between the effectiveness of schools.

| Termly plan  Spring  First half term | Subject  Science | Year  R 1 2 3 4 5 ⑥ |
|---|---|---|
| **Coverage/focus (including PoS reference if approp.)**<br>Humans as Organisms: AT2<br>1 c/d/e. circulation<br>1f movement<br>1h health | **Cross-curricular themes**<br>Fitness: data<br>Ourselves: movement<br>Sound/Light | **Resources**<br>Video/Classroom Assistant<br>Book resource (County Lib)<br>Computer CD ROM |

| **Key learning objectives** | **Activities and investigations** | **Cross-curricular links** |
|---|---|---|
| To understand that humans have skeletons and muscles & that these help them move<br><br>To understand the functions of the heart & its circulation<br><br>To appreciate the effects of exercise on the heart/pulse rate<br><br>To make decisions and to work with increasing independence | ① Brainstorming of the topic/key lesson 'you are one walking marvel'<br>② CD ROM — investigations on the skeleton — write ups 1st/2nd drafts<br>③ Labelling work of a skeleton/jigsaw/word search<br>④ AT1 Fitness test: group work<br>⑤ Pendown work on skeleton/FLARE body pictures<br>⑥ Handmaking to show the work of joints and tendons<br>⑦ Handout sheets (x2) on muscles and tendons<br>⑧ Handwriting exercises. | English — reading for understanding<br> — comprehension<br> — handwriting<br> — info gathering<br>Maths — measuring/handling data<br>PE — fitness muscle awareness<br>IT — Pendown Flare<br>Art — pencil drawings, computer graphices<br><br>**Key Elements for assessment this term**<br>Position and function of different parts of the body<br>AT1 Fitness Test<br>Whole topic assessment in prep for SATs |

FIG 3.1
Medium-term planning

## Short-term planning

A common problem with whole-school planning is the short-term plan. Teachers frequently have colour coded lever-arched files showing all the content that they are going to attempt during the course of the half-term. The links are established. The resources defined. When asked for daily and weekly plans however, some teachers use huge files, some use diaries, some use loose paper, some, we fear, use the back of envelopes. All of them plan — you couldn't go into a classroom and survive the week without knowing beforehand what you were actually going to do — but the process is not systematic and therefore there is no commonality about the structure as a whole and, crucially, few teachers routinely identify learning objectives.

The following example of short-term (daily) planning (p. 75) has been adopted by a number of schools. The effect of the introduction of this planning map has been immediate and dramatic. Short-term planning is now enjoyed by many of the staff mainly because they find it useful, manageable and it has direct and positive results on the quality of their teaching. Your colleagues, too, will see the need for relevant short-term planning initiatives, because they will see it as an aid to raising standards. Crucially, any short-term plan needs to be systematic to remain relevant.

Any school wishing to start looking at their short-term planning needs to adhere to the following links

**National Curriculum**
↓
**Content**
↓
**Learning Objectives**
↓
**Assessment**
↓
**Target Setting**

Plans need to be examined weekly by the headteacher and seen on a termly basis by the three core subject leaders and perhaps half termly by the deputy head teacher. The rationale behind the weekly planning sheet is to ensure that lesson content relates to the National Curriculum and that ICT (information and communications technology) runs through all the core subjects (indeed can now be regarded as one of four core subjects).

The weekly planning sheet should give instant access to curriculum coverage and leads very easily on to the daily planning sheets such as Figure 3.2. Each page is three sections. The first section is teaching method. Mortimer's seminal research, referred to earlier, showed just how important teaching methods were to pupils making progress.

> (the) effects were most positive when the teacher geared the level of work to pupils' needs, but not where all pupils worked on exactly the same piece of work . . . We found evidence that pupils gained from having lots of communication with the teacher. Thus those teachers who spent higher proportions of their time not interacting with the children were less success-ful in promoting progress and development . . . We are not, however, advocating traditional class teaching. Our findings do not show any such approach to be beneficial for pupils and in fact, we found no evidence of readily identifiable teaching styles at all. We feel that teaching is far too complex an activ-ity for it to be categorised in this way. On the contrary our re-sults indicate the value of a flexible approach, that can blend individual, class and group interaction as appropriate.
>
> (Mortimer et al. 1993, pp. 14–15)

OFSTED have identified the importance of teaching style and encouraged teachers to examine the 'fitness for purpose' of the methods chosen. If using such planning sheets teachers are required to identify the teaching style they will use, the head teacher can see that teaching style has been considered, teachers can check back and see the way they have been more and less successful during the term and anyone taking over at short notice knows what to expect in terms of class organisation.

You will find that helping teachers to define learning objectives is the hardest part of leading planning activities.

**Daily Planning Sheet**

Week beginning _____

| IW — Individual Work |
| RW — Research Work |
| PW — Paired Work |
| GW — Group Work |

| CL — Class Lesson |
| CM — Curriculum Manager |
| *Note: No listings denotes whole class teaching* |

Monday

| Teaching Method | Learning Objectives | Evaluation |
|---|---|---|
| GW<br><br><br><br><br>PW | Handwriting — correct letter formation and improve work presentation<br>Maths — find totals of money, work out how to pay, give change<br>Art — respond imaginatively to a story<br>Story — Listen attentively<br>Read with expression + fluency | I am unsure what we are achieving in handwriting practise — I am certainly failing to correct problems with wrongly formed letters and therefore problems are being re-inforced. The staff need to discuss beginning joined writing in Key Stage 1. |

Tuesday

| Teaching Method | Learning Objectives | Evaluation |
|---|---|---|
| PW<br><br>GW<br><br><br><br><br><br>IW | Develop links with parents and supporting children in maths games<br>English — prepare suitable questions to find out what is involved in Deputy Head's job<br>Maths — apply numeracy skills in mixed questions<br>Geography — recognise attractive/ unattractive features around school<br>Read independently | The regular test practise in maths is very successful and skills of applying knowledge are improving — more test variety would be helpful. |

FIG 3.2
Daily planning sheet

Your colleagues will probably find identifying content from the National Curriculum relatively easy now that they have had 10 years of experience. However, being sufficiently precise about what they actually want the children to learn will possibly be more of a problem. This, too, will need practice. Coordinators could encourage their colleagues to write down the learning objectives on a daily basis. The learning objectives may be taken directly from the National Curriculum Programmes of Study. An alternative approach is to use the NC as a base but just think what is it that Sally will know, be able to do, be able to do better, quicker, more consistently, by the end of the lesson than she could before it? Will this be the same for all children in the class or do we need to define slightly different learning objectives for all, for most, and for some children in the class? If your staff are still having difficulty, tell them that the LEA has stopped paying them an annual salary but has devolved responsibility for teachers' wages to the children. Each pupil has the power to pay their teacher 50p per hour if they learn what you have set them to learn. The teacher's task is to tell the children what they will learn, teach them it and then assess if they have learned it. If the kids don't learn the teachers don't eat. This tale has the effect of sharpening up students' responses to the problem of defining learning objectives. See if it does the same for your staff.

In order to encourage teachers to consider the success and otherwise of their teaching the heading 'evaluation' appears on the right-hand side of each daily planning sheet (rather than the word assessment). This section can be quite telling. For instance, if a member of staff evaluates a lesson as less effective because the computer has still not been fixed there is a lesson to be learned. However, the main reason for this section on evaluation is to allow teachers the time, the space and the structure to evaluate what is going on in their lessons. When this initiative was first started teachers in some schools were guilty of writing down things like 'This was a good lesson'. Now having had practice over the last year, teachers generally evaluate the lesson quality by looking at how many children have succeeded in achieving the learning objective.

All you have to do in short-term planning is to provide a structure that identifies teaching style, learning objectives and gives the opportunity for the teacher to assess how well or not pupils are performing. It isn't necessary to cover every detail. This ensures not only a systematic school-wide approach, because everybody's presenting their plans in the same way, but it also gives a clear indication to the headteacher and senior members of staff just what the teachers intend.

It also gives subject coordinators and other senior staff a chance to develop a whole-school perspective by scrutinising the relevant detail for that particular term. In such a school the typical OFSTED inspector's question to coordinators 'How do you know what's going on in school in your subject?' will be answered 'I have access to the planning books'. If this is followed up by 'and what about the standards?' such teachers may also answer that they collect samples of children's work (see Chapter 7).

As assessment coordinator, you may need to ask how closely do teachers conform to the school's policy, do they meet the agreed schedule, is assessment data being used to inform lesson planning? You cannot be indifferent to the quality of planning which takes place in your school. Without good planning teachers have no justification in assessing children at all. Imagine if after your next in-service day you end by testing the participants on the German vocabulary or the reasons for the Russian Revolution. They would rightly complain that you have not been teaching this. Pupils would be right to object if assessment was not preceded by carefully thought-out teaching to the learning objectives appropriate to the subject under question. Hence planning is a vital prerequisite to assessment, planning for assessment is necessary for good quality results and planning to use the results makes the whole process worthwhile.

Next we turn to the way in which we establish this good practice across the curriculum.

| Chapter 4 | Establishing assessment practice across the curriculum |

❝ *We pass through the world only once. Few tragedies can be more extensive than the scrutiny of life, few injustices deeper than the denial of an opportunity to strive or even hope, by a limit imposed from without but falsely identified as lying within.*

(Gould, 1981, p. 29)

The plain truth of the matter is that the more teachers are involved in the assessment of children's work the better they become at it. They improve in accuracy, their confidence grows and the process takes up less of their time. Thus assessment coordinators have to find ways to encourage their colleagues to practice levelling work and to discuss their judgments against those made by other teachers. You therefore need to try to set up a range of initiatives which will provide staff with a systematic assessment model that they all understand and use on a regular basis.

The particular assessment model advocated here links with the assessment overview shown earlier but, in any case, your school will need to have adopted a version of the following:

- **Assessment policy**   to provide a structure

- **Portfolios**   to help teachers make accurate judgments; to provide evidence and ensure consistency;

|   |   |   |
|---|---|---|
|   |   | to become a reference point;<br>to provides a means of monitoring the assessment policy;<br>to give opportunities for assessment. |
| ■ | **Records of Achievement** | to help children to set targets;<br>to develop children's ability to be critical;<br>to celebrate achievement;<br>to involve parents. |
| ■ | **Assessment folders** | to provide a systematic structure<br>to record regular on-going teacher assessment;<br>to provide evidence for summative assessment;<br>to show progression. |

❝ *Assessment and record keeping have always been a part of a primary teacher's work. They are powerful and important because it is the assessment that teachers make about pupils' progress that allows them to plan and make provision for individual children's development. This is the crux of formative assessment.*                                      (Sue Pidgeon, 1992)

The introduction of the National Curriculum brought with it tick sheets and charts, spread sheets and 'rainbow sheets', high-lighting charts and assessment books that had a discouraging effect on classroom teachers. The result has been that some teachers have seen assessment as the master of the curriculum and not its servant. The coming of the National Curriculum should have made the purpose of assessment much clearer but,

❝ *What was once the teacher's delight in informal assessment has turned into a legal responsibility and an administrative challenge for the entire school.*           (Rosalind Goodyear, 1990)

The aim of this chapter is to help you to provide that purpose so that your classteacher colleagues can use a variety of assessment techniques across the curriculum, but at the same time being realistic in what they should and could be assessing.

**Think about:**
Observing children as they work
Talking to them about their work
Looking at their workbooks and folders
Looking at classroom displays
Looking at school records
Talking with teachers about children's progress
    and achievements
Looking at their portfolios of achievements
Looking at performance profiles as reflected by
    test results
Involving children in some self-evaluation
Using questionnaires to teachers and/or pupils
(Newton and Newton, 1998, p. 164)

# Informal assessment

Informal assessment includes those 'spur of the moment' judgments made about a child as he or she is working in the classroom and the on-going tests and assessments made as a result of marking work or engaging in the activities described by Newton and Newton (1998). A problem with on-going assessments is that teachers may feel at one extreme that every exercise has to be levelled or at the other that they need do none at all. Thus the assessment overview earlier is intended to give staff the confidence to know what and when they should assess so that they can get on with the job of teaching. The school's assessment policy should lay down the actual number of informal assessments that have to be made each term.

The prototype policy in this book stipulates three per subject. Is this enough? Three mathematics assessments per term equates to nine per year. Nine per year means 54 assessments across the primary age range. That's surely enough to show progression and achievement. Nine assessments per year sounds a lot, but through experience we know that it is manageable. To better understand this process let us take English as an example.

There is now so much commercial assessment material available to help teachers make judgments in English that many English coordinators regard it as a waste of time for individual teachers to design their own work sheets, in order to ascertain the level a child has obtained. With Reading (EN2) most teachers will, of course, listen to individual children read, but with the introduction of the literacy hour, unless schools find the extra time for this activity it will probably not happen to the same extent and in the same ways as previously. Children will regularly read in groups with the teacher. In order for the child to be placed on a National Curriculum reading level that is relevant and up to date, there also needs to be individual teacher assessment.

There are a number of techniques. The basis of the end of Key Stage 1 reading task is *Miscue Analysis*. In this the child reads a set text under the guidance of the classteacher and the number of correctly read words can be translated to a reading level.

*Cliff Moon's Reading Assessment* makes the levelling of a child's reading stage even easier and can be linked to the above. The evaluation of the Miscue Analysis is fairly detailed — for instance 90 to 100 per cent of correctly read words would give a very high level of confidence in the set text and indicate that the child should be moved to the school's next reading stage. Moon makes the task of equating this to a reading level very easy.

*Levelled Comprehension Papers* are aimed at assessing the child's understanding of text and clearly link with the end of Key Stage SATs. In this part of the test many schools have pupils who score very high marks. These schools clearly prepare their children for the SAT tests. They do this by regular use of *Levelled Comprehension Papers* which are directly based on set SAT criteria.

*Published papers* (for example those produced by Letts) can be linked to the more formal assessment of children's work. Many teachers striving to improve their pupils' scores are now turning to such work. Often teachers only undertake parts of these papers which emphasise the learning objective planned for that lesson.

Using the *Reading Level Descriptors*. Great care needs to be taken with the direct use of level descriptors which may lead teachers to tick-lists. A way forward is to change these descriptors into 'Can dos' which not only will make the process more positive, but also involves the child in the assessment of their own work.

Through experience as a SATs marker it can be seen that with EN3, schools are now preparing their children for the tests and that regular practice in all writing forms has lead to teachers requiring assessment systems. These systems will help teachers quickly and effectively assess the work undertaken even by large classes of children.

**Level 1**

**Pupils can**:
- recognise familiar words in simple texts
- use knowledge of letters and sound-symbol relationships to read words
- read familiar words aloud and understand the meaning of what they read
- say what they like about stories, poems and non-fiction

**Level 2**

**Pupils can**:
- read simple texts (e.g. 'Frog and Toad are friends', accurately (with no more than 5 or 6 inaccuracies in a passage of 100 words)
- understand what they have read and be able to retell main points
- express an opinion about events and ideas in stories, poems and non-fiction
- use phonics to help them read words*
- can use word shape to help them read words*
- can use grammatical and contextual clues to help them read words*

* 'Some pupils rarely use more than one strategy. The important point is that pupils should be able to have recourse to more than one strategy and use another strategy when the first one fails'. (Assessment Office).

**Level 3**

**Pupils can**:
- read a range of texts (stories, poems, plays, dictionaries)
- read fluently (with few pauses) and with expression
- read accurately
- use a small range of strategies to read unfamiliar words
- show understanding of the main points of fiction and non-fiction texts
- say what they like about a book or a character
- express preferences in their choice of books
- use knowledge or the alphabet to locate books
- use an index and content list

'Please note that Level 3 is the last level at which pupils are expected to demonstrate competency in reading by reading aloud to the teacher or to other pupils. Fluency, accuracy and intonation are excluded from all subsequent level descriptions'. (Assessment Office).

**Level 4**

**Pupils can:**
- respond to a range of texts (see Level 3)
- show understanding of main ideas and themes in texts
- begin to draw logical conclusions (deductions)
- begin to advance ideas and theories (inference)
- use inference and deduction to comment on characters, features and actions
- refer to the text when explaining views
- locate ideas and information and use them in their discussions

**Level 5**

**Pupils can:**
- show understanding of a range of texts
- select points from a text to support arguments (sentences, phrases, information)
- draw logical conclusions using inference and deduction
- find information from a range of sources
- skim and scan where necessary
- draw together information from more than one source in a coherent way

## Agreement trialling

Schools have had the most effective assessment schemes at hand since 1995, namely the Key Stage 1 and Key Stage 2 Mark Schemes which are delivered to schools each year at the same time as the SAT papers. Many schools have not made best use of them. If used regularly, especially in whole-school agreement trialling, these schemes can give a structure to assessment, while at the same time benefiting teachers who become better practised at focusing on the elements necessary to improve their pupils' scores. The reason for this is simple — the mark scheme of the Key Stage 1 and 2 SATs signify the range and relative importance of the demands of the National Curriculum. Therefore, if, for example, the teaching of grammar is not adequately taught in your school, then children will probably be given a low 'grammar' mark by comparison to say their 'style' mark. This when known, will then inform any plan for improvement. In agreement trialling when the whole staff are looking at the work of a cohort of children, as the issues emerge, those who discover the 'problems' are the very people with the ability to do something about it.

In the chapter on Target Setting (Chapter 5) three examples of Key Stage 1 work are analysed, so here we will study in some detail the work of an older child. Figure 4.1 shows the story entitled 'The Open Box'.

As a start to whole school agreement trialling, you might encourage staff to read this piece of work and then from their knowledge of the National Curriculum discuss the presence and absence of the relevant features and give it a level.

The process of agreement trialling includes:
- background information;
- explanation of using the (in this case) narrative mark scheme;
- marking the work using the POGS (Purpose, Organisation, Grammar and Style) and
- explanation of key issues.

## Background information

In day to day classroom assessment this will not normally be necessary because the teacher will know the background to the lesson, the learning objectives and the strengths and weaknesses of the child. With whole staff agreement trialling it is advisable to at least 'set the scene' by describing:
The age of the child
The amount of teacher input
The learning objectives for this lesson
Whether this is the first, second or third draft piece of the work

In the case of 'The Open Box' the work was undertaken by a Year 6 boy in response to the famous war poster of Winston Churchill saying 'Forwards to Victory'. It was a piece of literacy work linked to history and life since the 1930s. There was no teacher input, except in the explanation of the learning objective, and the setting of frameworks, such as the establishing of time limits, etc.

Tuesday 14th March.

## The Open Box

I slowly opened the grey lid. There inside the big, grey box was an old 1920's suit. The suit was brown with an old fashioned look. There was a dark brown waist-coat, which flapped about, and smelt like pages of an old book. I put on the old suit, suddenly a strange feeling crawled all over my body. I said, "HELP, whats happening"? I

I tried to take the suit off but it was no good. It was stuck like glue! I pulled and I pulled, po but it would not come off.

Suddenly, there were white flashing lights and big, loud bangs. I must have passed out or something. When I woke up I was in a hospital bed with a big white bandage around my forehead, and I had

a heddache as though a ten ton weight
had slammed on my tiny little head.
I shouted for the nurse "NURSE!"
She came in as quick as a rabbit.
I said "Whats happened to me?"
The nurse replied:.
"When you were found we didn't know wh
you were."
Anyway, you have cut your head open.
and we have stitched it up. ¶
"Would you like an asprin at all?"
"No Yes please, My head is killing". So the
nurse got me an asprin and a drink of
coldwater. After about half an hour my
headache went and I started to walk
about for a bit. I felt dizzy, so I sat
down in a chair next to my bed.
I still had the suit on. "How come
you didn't take my suit off?" "We couldn't
take it off you its stuck on." I said
"Have you tried soaking me in a bath of
warm soapy water?" "Yes, but it was no
good." Said the nurse. Then a thought

came into my head, what if I have
travelled through time or something.
I remember a story about it once.
No, it can't happen, afterall time-
travel isn't possible. I asked the nurse
year it was just in case it did happen. The nurse what
said the year was 1923. I nearly
fainted when the nurse said it. I laid down
on the soft bed for a while. After about
an hour the nurse took the bandage
of my head, and said that I could
go. I wondered around for a bit to
see where I was. I asked a small
man where I was and he said
" Your in London, dear chap".
Well, at least I know my way around.
I felt around in my pockets and there
was a wallet in my pocket. I went
into a café and asked for a cup glass
of Pepsi." PEPSI! what's Pepsi?" said the
man behind the bar. Oops, sorry I will
have a cup of tea instead." Right that
will be 3p please." So I gave him the

87

the money and had my drink.
After that, I wondered down to the
houses of parliament. There was a
massive ~~crowed~~ crowd of people
around and a stand with a man talking
to ~~us~~. He said his name was Winston
Churchill. He was talking about how
dangerouse Germany was. He said
they were getting bigger tanks and
more aeroplanes. I started yelling questions
about what will happen in the future
I think everyone got a bit suspicious,
because everyone went quiet. The next
thing I knew was everyone was jumping
on me and saying he's a german spy!!
kill him. Suddenly that funny feeling
~~crawled~~ ~~ver~~ crawled all over my body
again, then there were flashing lights
and loud bangs. This time, I landed
on a soft bed in the loft. I was back home
I was jumping up and down on the bed.
I went down to my mum. She said, "I
"I thought you were cleaning out that loft
"You've only been up there a minute" "Mum's key!

FIG 4.1
Example of narrative for agreement trialling

## Using the Narrative Framework (mark scheme)

The crucial aspects of using POGS is to be familiar with all its aspects. Staff of many schools are now so familiar with agreement trialling and the mark framework, they now openly boast that they no longer read and use the scheme. The more teachers use the guide the better they become at quickly understanding key points, and aspects to search for. By studying this boy's story, your staff can become familiar with the same assessment processes that the key stage markers use every year in May/June when marking their basic 300 script allocation. Figure 4.2 shows elements of the Purpose and Organisation (QCA, 1998) part of the narrative mark scheme. If using this exercise to level 'The Open Box' with staff you should use the full scheme which has been sent to every school.

| Purpose and Organisation | |
|---|---|
| Just below LEVEL 3 | Some basic elements of story are present, including opening… More than one character… some story language… *One day… suddenly…* May be used                9 marks |
| LEVEL 3 | …story structure used to organise events… The writing has a beginning, middle and ending… Events are related to one another, though not necessarily well-paced… Imagination is shown by the inclusion of some detail                12 marks |
| LEVEL 4 | The writing is coherent and well paced… Events logically related… there is significant interaction between characters… Characterization is evident, for example, though direct or reported speech. The writing is lively and seeks to interest the reader 15 marks |
| LEVEL 5 | …a secure grasp of the chosen form… Elements of dialogue action and description are interwoven — such as opening with action or dialogue… the writer may show control of the dialogue… Thoughts and feelings of characters. Paragraphing may be used to mark main divisions…                18 marks |
| High LEVEL 5 | development of a theme as well as a plot… use of a non-linear time-line,… inclusion of conflict or relationship. Reflection on characters…        21 marks |

FIG 4.2
Elements of Purpose and Organisation

## The Use of POGS

The repeated use of POGS can rapidly increase teachers' skills in assessing and levelling children's written work. Through consistently using this system, your colleagues will become more familiar with what is required of them in teaching the National Curriculum. Most staff find it easier to mark the Grammar and Style section first, mainly because they can do both together after some practise. It becomes clear, for example, that in order to obtain Level 4/5 to the teacher needs find that:

- most sentences are correctly demarcated;
- the use of speech marks is evident with new speech starting on a new line;
- there is extended use of punctuation in evidence, such as question marks. (This is seen as important.);
- there is evidence of sentence connectives other than 'and' or 'then.' These could include 'because' 'if' and 'although';
- the use of adjectives are seen as an important form of description and
- the use of adverbs, such as 'quickly', are used to show effectiveness of the writing.

It also becomes clear to teachers (and markers) very early in this assessment process that many marks, be it in narrative or non-narrative writing, are awarded in the section on Purpose and Organisation.

There are five key areas associated with scoring high marks:

- that there is a clear beginning, middle and end and that the ending shows a clear grasp of 'finish';
- in narrative writing there needs to be a significant interaction between characters. To achieve this in the short term, teachers need actively to limit the number of characters children use.
- non-narrative writing has a clear idea of layout and a fitting conclusion;
- non-narrative writing should have good coverage of the main issues.
- In other words, the child needs to write a fair amount of text, establish a sense of audience and use paragraphing effectively.

Therefore, if we again refer to 'The Open Box' story shown in Figure 4.2 we can see that the marks awarded against the QCA mark scheme could be as follows:

| Grammar | 5 |
| Style | 5 |
| Purpose and Organisation | 15 |
| | 25 Total |

QCA have distributed to all primary schools a mark grid to convert total scores into National Curriculum levels. Twenty-five marks in the above example, equates to Level 4 in narrative writing. Teachers experienced in this sort of assessment would have levelled this piece of work in minutes mainly because levelling of children's work is not like marking. The teacher is not interested for this purpose in checking spelling patterns or correcting poor grammar. Levelling is far quicker because the teacher is only looking out for the key areas in the scheme.

Once teachers are familiar with the mark scheme the assessment process is inevitably faster. The process has a uniform structure and this allows the teacher to identify quickly a 'section' problem. This means that if Mary, writing the same 'The Open Box' story should score the following marks:

| Grammar | 5 |
| Style | 2 |
| Purpose and Organisation | 15 |
| | 22 Total |

the weakness of 'style' would be easily identified and can be addressed in future teaching. For example, her sentence connectives may need maturing so that she uses words like 'rather' or 'when'. Perhaps her stories need to contain more adjectives in order for her writing to become more lively. This form of assessment helps to identify such issues.

Similarly, detailed attention paid to assessment in other subjects will pay dividends. Coordinators of these subjects need to be encouraged to lead agreement trialling, develop staff skills and analysis in the same way. Help for coordinators in English and the other subjects of the curriculum may be found in a variety of books and official publications:

| Subject | Book and brochures for subject coordinators |
| --- | --- |
| English | Birch's (1995)* 'Coordinating English at Key Stage 1' and Ray's (1995)* 'Reading at Key Stage |

1' along with 'Reading the Changes' (Ray 1995a)** and Roberts' (1995)** 'Writing' provide help for coordinators who are starting to develop a leadership role in the Key Stage 1 and 2 curriculum. Additional assistance will be found in SCAA (1995a) *Consistency in Teacher Assessment: Exemplification of Standards, English.* Within this series, coordinators will find Tyrrell's (1999) *Coordinating English at Key Stage 1* and Waters and Martin's (1998) *Coordinating English at Key Stage 2.*

Mathematics   Brown's (1998) *Coordinating mathematics across the primary school* is the handbook within this series designed to help the mathematics coordinator. Additional recommendations are: Harrison, M. (1995a)** 'Working towards becoming the mathematics coordinator' and Stewart and Hocking's (1995) 'Directions in mathematics: the coordinator effect' will be useful for those just beginning in this role. Also of interest will be: OFSTED (1997) *The Teaching of Number in Three Inner-urban LEAs* and SCAA (1995b) *Consistency in Teacher Assessment: Exemplification of Standards,* Mathematics.

Science   Bowe's (1995)* 'The new science coordinator' and Cross and Byrne (1995)** 'Coordinating science at Key Stage 2' are of use to new coordinators. Within this series you will find Newton and Newton's (1998) *Coordinating science across the primary school.* For clarification of assessment SCAA (1995c) *Consistency in Teacher Assessment: Exemplification of Standards, Science.*

ICT   Tony Birch's (1995)* 'Developing the role of the Key Stage 1 IT coordinator: A case of the hare or the tortoise' and Harrison, M. (1995b)** 'Getting IT together in Key Stage 2' are relevant for newly qualified teachers or those new to their posts. In this series, Harrison's (1998) *Coordinating ICT across the primary school* and NCET (1992) *Assessing IT — Curriculum*

|           | *support materials* are of help along with SCAA (1997a) *Expectations in Information Technology.* |
|-----------|---|
| Geography | Boyle's (1995)** 'Providing a sense of direction in Key Stage 2' and Rodger's (1995)* 'Geography in the early years: the role of the subject manager' will be of help to those developing their leadership roles. In this series Halocha's (1998) *Coordinating geography across the primary school* is designed for coordinators as is SCAA (1997b) *Expectations in Geography.* |
| PE        | Chedzoy's (1995)* 'Developing a leadership role at Key Stage 1 — Physical Education' and Sanderson's (1995)** 'Physical education and dance: leading the way' are recommended for those new to the job. In this series, Raymond's (1998) *Coordinating physical education across the primary school* and the SCAA (1997c) booklet *Expectations in Physical Education* will be of assistance. |
| RE        | Bastide's (1998) *Coordinating religious education across the primary school* along with Mattock's (1995)** 'Religious education in Key Stage 2' and Mattock and Preston's (1995)* 'The Religious Education Coordinator' are recommended. |
| History   | Davies' (1995)* 'The history coordinator at Key Stage 1' and Davies' (1995a)** 'The history coordinator in Key Stage 2' will be useful to those starting to play this role. In this series, Davies and Redmond's (1998) *Coordinating history across the primary school* and SCAA (1997d) *Expectations in history* are more recent publications. |
| Art       | Piotrowski's (1995)** 'Coordinating the art curriculum in Key Stage 2' and Ray's (1995b)* 'Not Sunflowers again! Coordinating Art at Key Stage 1' will be useful chapters for NQTs and those new to the post to read. In this series, Clement, Piotrowski and Roberts' (1998) *Coordinating art across the primary school* |

should be read alongside SCAA (1997e) *Expectations in Art.*

| | |
|---|---|
| Design and Technology | Boekestein's (1995)* 'Tackling technology in the early years' and Cross' (1995)** 'Design and Technology at Key Stage 2' are useful chapters and, in this series, coordinators will find of use Cross' (1998) *Coordinating design and technology across the primary school* along with SCAA (1997f) *Expectations in Design and Technology.* |
| Music | Hennessy's (1998) *Coordinating music across the primary school* in this series and SCAA's (1997g) *Expectations in Music* will be of use to established coordinators and those developing their role will find useful Tony Walker's (1995)** 'Sounding the right note' and his daughter Rita Walker's (1995)* 'Starting off on the right note'. |

** denotes chapters from Harrison, M. (Ed) *Developing a Leadership Role in the Key Stage 2 Curriculum*
* denotes chapters from Davies, J. (Ed) *Developing a Leadership Role in the Key Stage 1 Curriculum*

## Record keeping

❛ *Many schools still have a burdensome and over-elaborate record-keeping system. There is a lot to be done before we achieve a consensus about an adequate and simple record-keeping process that:*
- *meets legal requirements;*
- *demands the minimum time and effort from teachers and*
- *ensures that the school collects and provides appropriate information for it to meet all its obligations.*

(Brown, 1998, p. 203)

Records should be useful, manageable, easy to keep and easy to interpret. It is not possible for teachers to record all their knowledge and they should not be tempted to try
(Sir Ron Dearing, DFE, 1994)

It need not be like this. The key areas in the development of a record keeping structure are:
trusting teacher judgments;
establishing a systematic whole school approach and keeping it simple.

**Records should be:**
Minimal: providing only information needed to maintain them.
Manageable: record systems should not involve great mountains of papers or be time consuming. They should support planning.
Meaningful: teachers should see record keeping as part of their teaching process and show continuation and progression.

(Harlen, 1983)

The example given in this chapter has worked well in a large number of primary schools, many of whom have been inspected recently. The process can, of course, be adapted to meet individual school needs, but basically consists of:

**An individual tracking document (shown in Figure 4.3)**

**A significant logging sheet as shown in Figure 4.4.**

All class assessment material would be kept in an assessment folder which may have the following basic structure.

**National Curriculum Record**

**Date**: Sept 1999   **Name**: Mary   **Year group**: 5

|      | Entry | TA | | | SAT NFER (SS) | Comment |
|------|-------|----|----|----|------|---------|
| En.1 | 2 | 3 | 3 | 3 | | |
| En.2 | 3 | 3 | 3 | 4 | 108 | Excellent reading S.S. |
| En.3 | 3 | 3 | 4 | 4 | | |
| EN. | 3 | 3 | 3 | 4 | | |
| Ma.1 | 2 | 3 | 3 | 4 | | |
| Ma.2 | 6 | 6 | 6 | 8 | 112 | Targeted 4 rules — excellent progression |
| Ma.3 | 3 | 3 | 3 | 3 | | |
| Ma.4 | 3 | 3 | 3 | 4 | | |
| MA. | 3 | 3 | 3 | 4 | | |
| Sc.1 | 8 | 8 | 8 | 8 | | |
| Sc.2 | 4 | 4 | 4 | 4 | | |
| Sc.3 | 3 | 4 | 4 | 4 | | |
| Sc.4 | 4 | 4 | 4 | 4 | | |
| SC. | 4 | 4 | 4 | 4 | | Extra targets in Yr6 to increase her to Level 5 |
| IT | 3 | 3 | 4 | 4 | | Individual log shows real understanding and very frequent computer experience |

FIG 4.3
An individual tracking document

## Assessment criteria

It is this section that helps teachers in their day to day assessment of children and is the main source for giving classroom teachers manageable strategies. It would contain the levelled writing examples given in the QCA 1998 mark scheme. The POGs would also be held here in order to help teachers with the assessment of writing. This section would also contain the 'Can dos' mentioned earlier in this chapter and also Cliff Moon's tables for converting reading ages to the National Curriculum levels. Thus the section contains all the elements which can help teachers to assess children's work. Many coordinators make sure that sheets in this section are laminated because of the wear and tear they will receive.

> *Am I supposed to know the levels that my children have obtained when they come to me as a new class?*
>
> (An anonymous teacher)

This remark was during a course run in London. The short answer, the only answer is — **yes**! Without the classteacher having the National Curriculum levels of all her new children in September, she cannot properly 'aim' the lesson content. Children coming into classes with no tracking document and therefore no NC levels means that their new classteacher will (and indeed must) pitch all levels for a few weeks at the average until he/she gets to know the levels of attainment of the children. This cannot be effective practice, but is unfortunately the norm in many schools.

A tracking document therefore needs to be set up, one which follows the child from Year 1 through to Year 6. The example shown in this book is a yearly document, started by the previous teacher in July when the entry level (entry into the new year) is filled in for all the attainment targets and IT. An example for Mary is shown in Figure 4.3 and would give the teacher a quick 'snap shot' of Mary's attainment as she enters Year 5. Thus on inspection it appears that Mary is generally performing at Level 3 in all areas except mathematics. The way the overall levels for the three core subjects are worked out are shown in the following section.

## English

Attainment Targets 1, 2 and 3 carry equal weighting.
Therefore, 3 add 4 add 3 totals 10. Divide 10 by 3 (the number
of attainment targets) and you arrive at Level 3 for the overall
entry level.

## Mathematics

Attainment Targets 1, 3 and 4 all carry an equal weighting, but
Attainment Target 2 is double weighted. This means whatever
AT 2 level has been given (in this case a Level 4) then this
becomes 8 marks (remember double weighting). Therefore,
we get this:

|      | Level |       |
| ---- | ----- | ----- |
| AT1  | 3     | 3     |
| AT2  | 4     | (8)   |
| AT3  | 4     | 4     |
| AT4  | 4     | 4     |
|      | **19**| **Total** |

This is divided by 5 (as AT2 is double weighted) which equals
a Level 4 (because you always level up).

## Science

AT1 in Science, according to QCA, is also double weighted, so
an initial Level 3 mark becomes 6 points. A total of 15 marks is
divided by 5, so Mary receives a Level 3.

|      | Level |       |
| ---- | ----- | ----- |
| AT1  | 3     | (6)   |
| AT2  | 3     | 3     |
| AT3  | 3     | 3     |
| AT   | 3     | 3     |
|      | **Total** | **15** |

Every term (Autumn, Spring and Summer) the classteacher
would enter the assessments for those attainment targets that
have been covered that term and produce an overall subject
level score. By the end of the academic year the teacher will
have a document that will have been updated regularly and
when a new tracking document is produced for the next

CE ACROSS THE CURRICULUM

QCA describe assessment within their scheme of work in IT for Key Stages 1 and 2:

*Where a child's progress differs markedly form the rest of the class, teachers may wish to make a note of this and the reasons for the difference. This provides a straightforward method for passing on information about children to the next teacher, without overly detailed records or bureaucratic systems of record keeping. The expectation set out at the end of each unit should assist in this process.*

(DfEE, 1998 p. 15)

academic year, the last attainment level in each core subject will be the entry level for the new year.

Furthermore, any testing, such as NFER Mathematics or reading scores can be added into the relevant box marked NFER/SS (standard scores). Teacher comments relating to Mary can be included at her discretion. The child will have a new sheet each academic year and the old document (there will be six in all) will be kept on the child's individual record card and follow the child to secondary school. These six sheets will be all that will be needed to plot the six years of a child's academic life at primary school.

The key to the above process is that classteachers become confident in recognising what it is that makes an English or Science Level 2 piece of work. This is in turn dependent on teachers' subject knowledge. Alongside all teacher agreement trialling and school portfolios the significant logging sheets are important in establishing quality teacher assessment (see Figure 4.4).

Significant logging sheets are the basic day-to-day recordings of children's achievements. They are designed to go into the assessment folder and each child has two sheets for each academic year. Principally, these are the main instrument that allows teachers to record achievements and then to fill in termly the tracking document.

The section entitled 'Other' would include data that the classteacher feels is important in establishing a picture of the whole child, however, these are **significant** logging sheets so only important assessment data needs to be recorded.

 *The records that arise from the assessment process should be selective and should identify and describe individual children's **significant achievements**. . . .*

(Brown, 1998, p. 203, his emphasis)

The section entitled 'Achievements' is there for teachers to record all that they feel is special about that child and would normally cover non-academic achievement. This might include playing in the school football/netball/swimming team; acting

| Pupil name | Task | Mark | Date |
|---|---|---|---|
| **Progress/remarks** | | | |
| | | | |
| | | | |
| | | | |
| | | | |
| | | | |
| | | | |
| **English** | | | |
| | | | |
| | | | |
| | | | |
| | | | |
| | | | |
| | | | |
| | | | |
| **Maths** | | | |
| | | | |
| | | | |
| | | | |
| | | | |
| | | | |
| | | | |
| | | | |
| **Science** | | | |
| | | | |
| | | | |
| | | | |
| | | | |
| | | | |
| | | | |
| **Other** | | | |
| | | | |
| | | | |
| | | | |
| | | | |
| | | | |
| **Achievements** | | | |
| | | | |
| | | | |
| | | | |
| | | | |
| | | | |

FIG 4.4
Significant logging sheet

as a house captain, being a member of the School Council or a form monitor. Maybe he or she produced the Year 6 play or eventually learned to swim 25 metres.

With the three sections each containing seven boxes and with the Assessment Policy stipulating three assessments per core per term, there would be a need for two sheets per child if regular progression is to be viewed at a glance. The core subject boxes, on the left, allow the teacher to write down quickly the basic background to the assessment e.g. was the piece of work first or second draft, was there significant teacher input, or was the science assessment part of the main yearly focus in AT 1.

The task undertaken by the child is recorded under 'Task' and could include the title 'Assessment', 'Number test', 'Data handling' or 'Non-narrative account'. The mark and the date are recorded to show achievement and progression. Such sheets are not only vital in producing a simple picture of the child's progress, but they are of great value for teachers when they have to inform parents of the child's performance in the core subjects. There is a clear need for teachers to become familiar with the correct terminology in order to discuss the core subjects.

The national literacy strategy uses terms such a metalanguage, antonym, assonance, calligram, cinquain, clerihew, haiku, genre, homophone, morpheme, renga, and trigraph. The science and mathematics subject knowledge may also be quite unfamiliar to your colleagues. The TTA have produced a series of training booklets and an accompanying CD ROM to assist with the development of teachers' subject knowledge in the core subjects and the National Grid for Learning at *http://www.ngfl.gov.uk/ngfl/about.html* is designed to serve teachers' needs.

Ultimately the Grid will be developed so that learners across the UK can access directly relevant information. Over the next year schemes of work for curriculum subjects; examples of high quality material used by practising teachers, such as school behaviour plans and individual education plans will be added to the site. In addition, there will be information

A poem made from *kennings* would be a list of expressions (naming something without using its name) such as:

My Dog
    *ankle biter*
    *bone cruncher*
    *night howler*
    *rabbit catcher*
    *fur pillow*
The National Literacy Strategy — p. 82
(DfEE, 1998b)

and guidance on government policy on a variety of subjects including: the national literacy and numeracy strategies; raising standards and effectiveness; school management; discipline and attendance; special educational needs; equal opportunities; under 5 provision and a section on out-of-school activities.

Thus coordinators of other subjects will need to be involved in staff development for the assessment policy to be effective.

## Chapter 5  Assessment leading to target setting

 *You don't have to be ill to get better.*

(Hopkins, Ainscow and West, 1994)

It seems that scarcely a day goes by without hearing someone setting one target or another on radio, on TV or in the papers. Targets to reduce NHS waiting lists; targets to reduce pollution; targets to increase crime detection; targets for schools. But any fool can set a target! This chapter aims to put target setting into perspective.

We maintain that it will only be those schools that have agreed effective assessment practices in place and teachers who use results systematically to inform teaching and learning which are likely to be successful in setting and achieving realistic targets. All schools, of course, are expected to have overall targets and a few may improve attainment just because they have been told that a certain percentage of their pupils are supposed to reach Level 4 in some subject or other by a certain date. This chapter will try to persuade you that everyone in your school should be target setting — not just the headteacher and governors — and that to be successful it is important for schools to develop a culture of goal setting, in accordance with the statutory target setting regulations about to come into force.

---

**Statutory target-setting in schools**

To all Head Teachers, Chairs of Governors and Chief Education Officers
20 May 1998

Dear Colleague

ANNOUNCEMENT OF STATUTORY TARGET-SETTING IN SCHOOLS

I am pleased to be able to give you more details on the today's announcement in Parliament about school based target-setting, following consultation earlier in the school year. Stephen Byers, the Minister for School Standards, announced that the relevant regulations will shortly be laid before Parliament which will require that Governing Bodies set and publish annual performance targets for 11 and 16 year olds.

Ministers believe that setting specific measurable targets at least once a year for pupil performance is a powerful lever for raising standards in our schools. This view was supported in the QCA consultation on target-setting. Target-setting should support school improvement and should not become a burdensome administrative procedure.

All maintained schools, including maintained special schools, with pupils at the appropriate ages will be required to set and publish in their governors' annual report to parents the following targets:

Key Stage 2: % of pupils attaining level 4 or above in English;

Key Stage 2: % of pupils attaining level 4 or above in mathematics;

Targets will have to be set each Autumn term, starting this year.

They must relate to those pupils who will take the National Curriculum tests towards the end of the following school year. This means setting targets this Autumn for 11 year olds' performance in Summer 2000. This is a change from the proposed requirement for targets to be set for 2000 and 2001, as indicated in the draft guidance on Education Development Plans (EDPs), reflecting Ministers' desire to ensure that administrative burdens are kept to a minimum.

Schools may want to augment these targets with others of their own choosing to reflect their particular priorities. In addition, schools should discuss indicative targets for future years as part of their dialogue with LEAs within the Education Development Plan process.

Best wishes

Michael Barber
Head of Standards and Effectiveness Unit          **(Edited version of Michael Barber's letter to schools)**

---

For target setting to become part of the school's general practice, assessment coordinators will need to discuss with their headteachers and teacher colleagues a number of issues which might reflect the following:

| Points for whole staff discussion | including | check |
|---|---|---|
| *Whether the whole staff has access to a range of sources of information on pupils' attainment and progress* | continuous teacher assessment<br>summative teacher assessment<br>end of key stage assessment results<br>QCA optional NC assessment results<br>baseline assessment information<br>the results of other tests the school uses (for example NFER standardised tests)<br>SEN reviews and,<br>assessments carried out by the language support services | |
| *How such information is recorded* | tracking sheets, RoA, reports to parents etc. | |
| *How the school currently uses the information it has gathered* | as a diagnostic tool for individual pupils<br>to monitor the quality of education it provides<br>    in IEPs<br>by focusing on particular groups<br>in differentiated curriculum plans<br>in subject reviews<br>through gender performance analysis<br>in the School Improvement Plan | |
| *Any constraints the school recognises in achieving the performance targets* | free school meals as an indicator of home background not contributing to educational progress<br>percentage of pupils on SEN register<br>pupil mobility<br>pupils with English as an additional language<br>the effects of a small cohort where one child represents a large percentage of the population<br>a concentration of any or all of these in one particular cohort | |
| *As a result of the above analysis, what is the best forecast the school can make about the National Curriculum levels pupils in the target cohorts will achieve* | as numbers and percentages for the next three years | |

Targets are like weather systems for they are neither solely 'top down' nor only 'bottom up'. The top affects the bottom e.g. the headteacher and the senior management team set targets for teachers and pupils and thereby raise expectations, and the bottom affects the top e.g. the children and the teachers set their own targets which will ultimately culminate in the school's overall attainment. Therefore, this chapter will concentrate on both school-level and class-level targets and also on class target setting.

# School level target setting

The 1997 Education Act stated that from September 1998 schools are required to:

- Set and publish pupils' performance targets annually
- Set targets in the core subjects of the National Curriculum

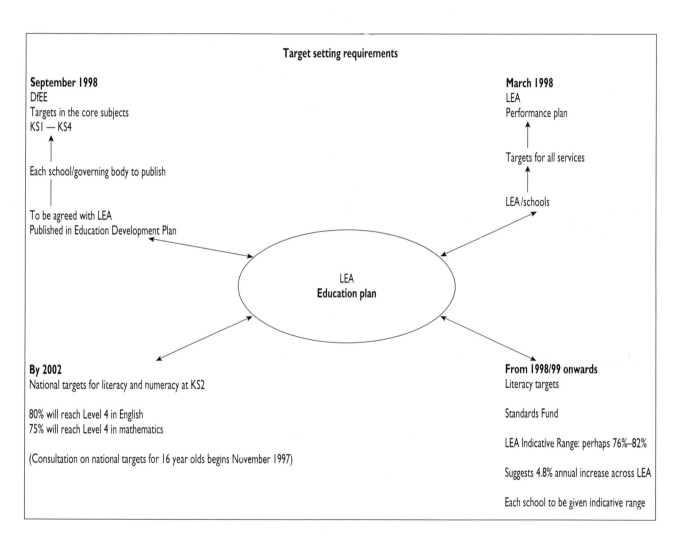

**Target setting requirements**

**September 1998**
DfEE
Targets in the core subjects
KS1 — KS4

Each school/governing body to publish

To be agreed with LEA
Published in Education Development Plan

**March 1998**
LEA
Performance plan

Targets for all services

LEA/schools

LEA
**Education plan**

**By 2002**
National targets for literacy and numeracy at KS2

80% will reach Level 4 in English
75% will reach Level 4 in mathematics

(Consultation on national targets for 16 year olds begins November 1997)

**From 1998/99 onwards**
Literacy targets

Standards Fund

LEA Indicative Range: perhaps 76%–82%

Suggests 4.8% annual increase across LEA

Each school to be given indicative range

Your LEA should provide guidance, analyse data, and help you to set realistic but challenging whole school targets for the next few years. LEAs have to include individual school's targets in their education development plans. The input that different LEAs provide will vary but teachers too must feel that they have a say in setting the literacy and numeracy targets for their schools otherwise this will become yet another exercise in which 'they' do things to 'us'.

However, as we claimed earlier, any fool can set targets. Headteachers and senior managers need a structure in place to obtain targets that are both meaningful and useful to their children and their staff. All targets set need to be

S   **s**pecific
M   **m**easurable
A   **a**chievable
R   **r**ealistic
T   **t**ime-related

Taken from *Targets to Action*, DfEE publication 1997.

Furthermore the process for target setting in school needs to involve all staff and governors by making sure all involved know what they need to do to achieve them; ensuring that practice is systematic throughout the school; and, making time available to complete the tasks involved.

School targets could simply read as a list for example:

## Targets for Swan Primary School 1999/2000

- To increase the number of children involved in extra-curricula activities by 25 per cent each year for four years
- By September 1999 to link the school with a high quality after-school play scheme
- By September 1999 to increase the opening hours of the school by fifteen hours a week and to be available as a community resource for 69 days during the holiday periods
- By September 1998 to link with parents in work or full-time education by providing a base for full-time child care and to be seen as a centre for training for NVQ trainers
- To improve achievement in English so that by the end of Key Stage 1 SAT results show that 90 per cent of children attain Level 2 or above
- By July 1999 to increase the number of pupils reaching or exceeding Level 4 in the three core subjects in KS2 to, English 65 per cent, mathematics 57 per cent, science 65 per cent

---

The judgment about when targets are **SMART** enough will be individual to each school but one can see that each of the following targets gets smarter in its refinement over the previous one.

*'I'm going to lose weight'*
*'I will start my diet soon'*
*'I will begin to diet tomorrow'*
*'I intend to begin the Weight Watchers' diet from tomorrow'*
*'I want to lose 2 stones'*
*'I want to get down to 13 stones'*
*'I intend weigh 13 stones by Christmas Eve'*

- To increase SAT results in KS2 from 1999 by 10 per cent over the next two year period
- By July 1999 to have no Year 6 children below Level 3 in English or mathematics (except those having a special educational needs statement)
- By Autumn term 1999 to have built an ICT room (without new PCs) that will be used on a weekly basis by all children
- January 1999, to have developed a system of quality short-term planning that identifies teaching styles, learning objectives and teacher assessment
- By October 1998 to have baseline assessment in place
- By December 1999 to have in place a planned programme of data to be used to increase pupil performance especially with boys in English En3
- By Easter 1999 to have established a high quality assessment policy that leads to target setting both in year groups and for individual children
- To build up links with local community bodies over the course of two years.

All those targets would have been agreed by the whole-school staff and by various committees of the governing body. Many are **smart** targets. They are specific. Nearly all of them are measurable (we will be able to tell if they've been successfully met). They are all certainly achievable in the opinion of staff and the governors who have had full involvement in the process, and, therefore, realistic in terms of quality and time. Most of them have some form of time limit. Target setting on this level can provide the headteacher and senior management team with a good early basis for their development planning. But this is hardly rocket science!

There are certain criteria that headteachers and governors need in setting the KS2 SAT forecasts, particularly in literacy and numeracy. To set targets that relate to the school's current position headteachers need to consider:

- previous years' results;
- national and LEA benchmarks;
- national and LEA ambitions; and
- teacher forecasts for the target cohorts.

At St Peter's CE Primary School in Salford each member of teaching and non-teaching staff acts as a personal tutor to one of a small number of Year 6 pupils. The pupils targeted are those the school hopes, with extra tuition and their own hard work, may achieve Level 4 in English by the end of the year. Tutors offer help and encouragement over their final year at especially arranged meetings.

This scheme is proving successful.

## Table 3: Schools with less than 50 per cent EAL and 21–35 per cent eligible for FSM

Percentage of children achieving Level 2 and above

**English**

| English | | 95 Percentile | | Upper Quartile | | Median | | Lower Quartile | |
|---|---|---|---|---|---|---|---|---|---|
| Teacher Assessment | | 94 | 92 | 85 | | 77 | | 68 | |
| Reading Test/Task* | | 95 | | 85 | 82 | 77 | | 67 | |
| Writing Test | | 96 | 94 | 86 | | 77 | | 67 | |

**Mathematics**

| Mathematics | | | | | | | | | |
|---|---|---|---|---|---|---|---|---|---|
| Teacher Assessment | | 98 | 96 | 90 | | 82 | | 74 | |
| Test | | 100 | 92 | 90 | | 82 | | 73 | |

**Science**

| Science | | | | | | | | | |
|---|---|---|---|---|---|---|---|---|---|
| Teacher Assessment | | 100 | 94 | 92 | | 84 | | 75 | |

Number of schools = 2,937

### How to use the table

The blank spaces in the table allow you to insert the appropriate results from your school.

For example, if 80 per cent of pupils reached Level 2 or above in the reading test/task, this places the school in the top 50 per cent of all schools in the table (above the median), and below the best performing 25 per cent (the upper quartile).

### Definition of terms used in the table

EAL: The percentage of children for whom English is an additional language. This is based upon the number of children of compulsory school age with English as a second language in form 7.

95 percentile: The performance exceeded by 5 per cent of schools.

Upper quartile: The performance exceeded by 25 per cent of schools.

Median: The performance exceeded by 50 per cent of schools.

Lower quartile: The performance below which 25 per cent of schools fall.

Number of schools: The number of schools with results used in this table. There are 2,937 schools with 21 to 35 per cent of pupils known to be eligible for FSM and less than 50 per cent EAL pupils, which returned Key Stage 1 results.

*Reading test/task: Pupils achieving Level 2 or above in the reading test/task are those achieving Level 2 or above in the reading test, plus those achieving Level 2 in the reading task but failing to reach Level 2 in the test.

FIG 5.1
Benchmarking (DfEE, 1997)

Let's take mathematics as an example. For schools to set a realistic target for children's achievement in mathematics it means that the previous two to three years' whole-school scores need to be compared with the corresponding national results. Staff and governors need then to study carefully teacher assessment forecasts made at the start of the year in question (this is why it is so important for all teachers making professional judgments to have assessment tracking documents for all children). LEA ambitions also need to be taken into account. These may state that the school needs to gain on average 2 percentage points over the next year and for each of a further four years after that. Nationally, this growth may be 3.5 per cent after the corresponding time span. The above list gives schools the credible information they need to be confident in establishing clear and challenging targets.

Furthermore, schools are now in a position whereby their pupils' attainment can be compared with those of (nearly) comparable schools. The benchmarking of schools with another similar school can help raise teachers' expectations. The two key indicators in this initiative are:

■ the proportion of children who are entitled to free school meals;
■ the number of children with English as an additional language.

The benchmarking chart (Figure 5.1) has been produced by the DfEE (1997) in order to help schools identify which quartile their school falls into, while at the same time identifying similar schools in their region. The school given as an example has 28 per cent children on free school meals and very few children with English as a second language.

Thus by using benchmarking data teachers can start to compare themselves with other schools which have a roughly similar intake of pupils.

*Targets into Action* (DfEE, 1997) demonstrates that given such data schools can embark on a five stage improvement programme.

| Stage | Key question | Summary |
|---|---|---|
| **Stage 1**<br>**Analysis** | *How well are we doing?* | Here the school is encouraged to look critically at its current achievement and consider trends; differences in performance between boys and girls, differences between achievement in different core subjects and in the attainment targets of the same subjects. |
| **Stage 2**<br>**Benchmarking** | *How well should we be doing?* | This is the point at which the school can compare itself with other (roughly) similar schools. All schools will receive Performance and Assessment reports (PANDAs) which place their schools in bands with schools whose intakes are judged socio-economically similar. It will be possible for schools to compare themselves against these others. |
| **Stage 3**<br>**Target setting** | *What more can we achieve?* | At this stage the school is seen as setting itself challenging but realistic targets. DfEE describes targets in the historic, the comfort, the challenging and the unlikely zone.<br><br>It is more than likely that the LEA will encourage you to set targets within the challenging zone. |
| **Stage 4**<br>**Action to improve performance** | *What must we do to make this happen?* | The DfEE admits that setting targets in themselves will not raise standards. Action is needed for schools to achieve the targets they have set. This may involve changing aspects of teaching; the curriculum; the time spent by pupils learning key skills; the involvement of parents; the resources; the use of teaching and non-teaching staff etc. |
| **Stage 5**<br>**Review of achievement** | *What have we done?* | At this stage the school has a chance to evaluate what they have achieved and begin the cycle again. |

Several schools have been successful in raising achievement through target setting and lessons have been learned through the study of those who have had difficulties. Ralph Tabberer, Tim Hine and Simon Gallacher (1996) looked closely at 31 primary schools taking part in a target-setting initiative in Staffordshire. They identify seven obstacles to effective target setting:

1 **Focusing uniquely on process targets rather than outcome targets**

Process targets are those concerned with changing school policy, procedures, teacher behaviours or other schooling processes rather than concentrating on pupil achievement. This can lead to a feeling that teams of teachers have been successful (after all they have adopted the new mathematics scheme, instituted a daily twenty minute silent reading period, written a science policy) without affecting pupil outcomes at all. Thus such schools, for all their effort, have not associated 'improvement' with impact on their children.

2   **A determination to improve outcomes is not complemented by the changes needed to make this happen**
   School processes have to be changed in step with outcome targets otherwise the over concentration on outcomes may lead to a narrow range of work which only addresses the measurable outcomes of the target. For example, a school may sets a target that pupils' reading ages as measured on test 'x' will be increased by 'y' by the end of the year. If no reading processes are changed to underpin this desire then, presumably, if the children are sent home with the words of test 'x' as spellings to learn every week for a year and consequently the target is achieved and the school will be satisfied with the result! School planning, involving aspects as diverse as resources, teaching techniques, time tabling and homework needs to make the change happen.

3   **Setting too many outcome targets**
   Confused rather than concentrated effort results from an attempt to fix everything at once. Just as development planning needs to set priorities so does the process of target setting.

4   **Setting targets in the wrong 'zone'**
   Some primary schools in this study set *historic* targets, that is goals they had already achieved in an attempt to 'domesticate' a process which they perceived as threatening. These schools had no impact on raising children's achievement. Beyond the historic zone some schools set targets in the *comfort* zone, a little ahead of what they were achieving already, and others further ahead the *smart* zone, using the **smart** formulae above. Finally ambitious schools may set *unlikely* zone targets which are so high that they invite failure. Success has, of course, been achieved with 'unlikely' targets and some headteachers have deliberately set such targets (see Dame Tamsyn Imison's (1998) account of her targets for Hampstead Comprehensive) but this strategy is usually associated with stress and high risk.

5   **Setting improvement targets inappropriate to the needs of their pupils**
   Research evidence found that some schools set targets such as increasing the proportion of pupils reaching Level 3 at

age seven (elite targets); others improving the average score in reading tests (cohort targets) and yet others in achieving zero failure (reliability targets). Unless schools understand the effect on pupils left out of such targets they will not be able to make the appropriate choices for their own sets of pupils.

6  **Getting the psychology of target setting wrong**
Targets set from the outside frequently are met with active or passive resistance. There needs to be a balance between accountability so that the targets are taken seriously and support so that people are helped to achieve them.

7  **Not following targets through**
If most of the year is spent in review, planning and target setting and this leaves little time for enactment then all target setting has done is to create another diversion.

## Class target setting

So several benefits may be gained from whole-school target setting. However, we've no doubt that if target-setting is to lead to raising standards then the real energy of staff and governors needs to be focused on the quality of classroom processes. It is only in the classroom where effective improvement in children's learning takes place. With this in mind schools are moving on from simply grading each child's levels of competence (e.g. Level 2B for English narrative story writing or Level 3 for number) to using such assessments to set agreed targets with children on how they can improve; how they can move to another level.

It is important that staff understand the central role of regular target setting with children. An exercise assessment coordinators might use with their colleagues is to use the examples of three children's work given below. As part of a course on effective target setting teachers are often encouraged to look at each of these pieces of work and then attempt to award a NC level to each piece. Example 1 is a narrative called

'Stuck' written by a Year 2 boy in January 1998. There was no teacher input and the example given is his first draft. The learning objective for this piece of work was writing to convey a meaning with detail and to show evidence of sentence construction.

## Stuck

Fred Went to School. When He got to School. He Sat down nex to chris. The teacher Said we are doing a . test and Fred copied chris. chris did not tell she teachher but She Saw him capied chris. Then it came to playtime and Fred had to Stop it.

The second piece of story writing called 'The Broken Pencil' was written by a Year 2 girl, again in January 1998. The piece was second draft with very little in the way of instruction except for the initial introduction and prompt. The child took 25 minutes to write the story. The learning objective for this piece of work was 'to use sufficient detail to make the story interesting to the reader and to show evidence of understanding'.

## The broken pencil

One day We Went to School. I Was
new in the School. I b̶r̶o̶t̶ bought Some
pencil's. The pencils Were Very
lite. Mr Joe our teacher said
We could have them to draw
with. I Sat down on a gray chair.
We did draw with the pencils.
I looked at the class room.
It Was like a very big Forest
Then Some one broke one of
my pencils. I cryed my eye's out.
Mr Joe Said you will be very
bize like an ant. Because you will
have to get it up. So the tall
boy how Was like an elephant
did.

The third piece of story writing was completed by a boy in
Year 2 and then copied onto the computer using Words for
Windows. The work was done in November 1998 and was
uncorrected and unaided by his class teacher. The learning
objectives were 'trying to show a growing awareness of
punctuation and showing some features of narrative style'.

*Suggestion*

Using these three examples level them yourself and then consider targets for improvement for each child.

Take them to a staff agreement trialling session and repeat the exercise with groups of teachers.

---

Tuesday 25th November

The Paper Doll

One day me Richard and Ashley were building a paper doll at school. Everyone had to make one in a three. When we'd built it we hung them on the wall. Then everyone had finished we had to do maths after. It was dinnertime everyone went for dinner. When me and Ashley had finished we waited for Richard. Richard finished we went in the classroom to look at the paperdoll. We found it walking around in the classroom. It went to the book shelf to read a book. It red the tinder box. Then it red clarans clowns we tried to catch it but it was too fast and it jumped alot of times. At last we cort it it was fun to catch it When school had finished me Richard and Ashley asked our mums and dads if theyed take us to black park? they said yes. We took the paper doll on pepsimax and lots of uther rides we slept in the caravan in the morning we went home.

---

From this position where your teachers now know the learning objectives and the background information, the readers are invited to level these pieces of story writing.

Key Stage 1 teachers should be using writing performance descriptions for Levels 1 and 3, published by QCA (1998). Using this performance data staff might be encouraged to level each of these pieces of work.

It is our experience that most teachers come to agreement far better when they are sitting in groups discussing hypotheses and testing judgments against one another than if they were required to do so in isolation. The consensus develops well if the time to do the exercise is limited.

When originally assessed these pieces of work were given the following grades by the class teacher:
    Example 1 was given a 2C
    Example 2 was given a 2B
    Example 3 was given a 2A

Hundreds of teachers have now worked with these examples and no one has ever given example 1 a 2A and no one has ever given example 3 a 2C. This shows a convergence of interpretations of the programme descriptions. (There were a number of teachers in London that gave example 3 a Level 3.) Example 2 appears to pose the most problems, although example 3 (the word processed story) tends to be difficult to judge because of the lack of personalised handwriting. It can be the case that some teachers tend to be influenced by a good handwriting style and this confirms their judgments.

Once the levelling has been accomplished it is now standard practice in many schools to consider setting specific targets for improvement based upon the judgments they have made. Many schools encourage teachers to talk to each other and to finalise either one, two or three targets. The following targets were identified by the classteacher as appropriate for the children whose work is given in the three examples above.

Example 1, Level 2C — targets for development
■ accurate use of capital letters and full stops
■ not mixing lower and upper case letters e.g. 's'
■ extending writing — more events and developing endings

Example 2, Level 2B — targets for development
■ correct use of full stops and capital letters throughout the writing
■ spelling — recall of letter strings e.g. ght
■ develop skills in using descriptive words

Example 3, Level 2A — targets for development
■ consistent use of full stops and capital letters
■ use of speech marks and question marks

Putting these targets together it is clear that there is a thread running through each child's work: the need for future teaching about punctuation skills. Thus here is an example of assessment leading to future planning. Teachers will set targets for individual children in a number of areas but if a number of children are examined closely it may be the case that there will be a thread that can identify a need for curriculum planning.

Marking is an effective way to keep a child focused on agreed targets and this is the way that the child makes sense of their learning. With this in mind, it's no surprise to many experienced teachers that the most effective assessment and

FIG 5.2
Assessment and target setting

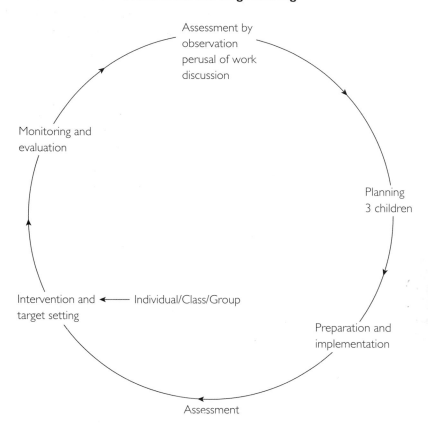

**Assessment and target setting**

target setting is done with the cooperation of the child concerned. This means that the teacher should be free to make decisions about when, who and how to mark.

Effective assessment and target setting should have as its base the structure shown in Figure 5.2.

There are three types of assessment in the classroom. One is the teacher observing her class or individual children and the second, and perhaps most important, is the scrutiny of work and the third one is discussion — sitting down with the children and discussing what they understand and what they can and cannot do. Some coordinators say you should be doing this with perhaps as many as six children. Coordinators might try this for themselves before advising their colleagues about how many to try at once. Our advice is to start with three. You only have to try this to realise that more is impractical and won't work. It is simply too time consuming and unmanageable.

However, once those children have been identified, teachers can then prepare and implement the teaching activities that have been planned. Once a target has been attained (or the teacher feels a change is needed) then the teacher adds another target. It is then up to the teacher to assess the learning of such children and, as we've stated already in this chapter, one of the most effective forms is sitting down with the child and going through their work. Then of course the teacher monitors the class and individual and evaluates how well the lesson has worked and then highlights any needs in future assessment for different types of teaching content.

## A further INSET activity

The Year 3 work example a 'A Guide to Flamborough' (p. 119) is a second draft piece of work that has as its learning objective the ability to extend ideas logically and an attempt to write in an organised fashion. Coordinators might choose to use this piece of work with teachers wishing to understand and learn about the impact they can have on a daily/weekly basis.

Coordinators should divide their colleagues into groups of at least four. One person should be selected to take on the role of the child, who we will call Sabhir, whose work will be examined and one teacher will take on the role of Sabhir's teacher. The remaining group participates using the intervention skill sheet shown in Figure 5.3 (p. 120).

This process is very powerful in showing staff the skills needed to achieve sound intervention. There is no great secret, indeed most of it is simple common sense backed up by knowledge of the child and knowledge of how children learn. There's little doubt that work done with teachers to improve their intervention skills requires the following points.

Good teacher intervention requires:
■ that the teacher is clear about which children she is going to observe, how and when she is going to intervene

# A Guide to Flamborough

Over a thousand years Ago
after the romans the vikings
Came across the north
sea to invade Britain.
They came from Denmark
thats Why they were

Danish raiders the vikings
Were very greedy. Flamborough
has a lovely seaside and
lots of nice craftshops
When the vikings came across the north
sea they had come from Flamborough.
They had Just invaded Flamborough so they
wanted to invade Britain.

Fish dolpin

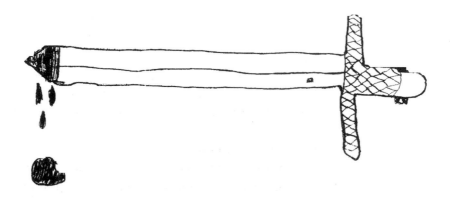

**Observer's checklist**

Score by marking a point on the line with a cross | **Yes** | **No**

**The trainer's opening comment:**

Was it    positive?

communicated sincerely?

focused on an aspect of the learner's work?

**The correction:**

Was it    clearly explained (demonstrated)?

communicated objectively
(i.e. without personal judgment)?

Communicated openly
(i.e. good eye contact, open posture, etc.)?

**The closing comments:**

Were they    positive?

communicated sincerely?

focused on improvement of the learner's work?

clear in setting a relevant and attainable target?

FIG 5.3
Intervention skills

© Bishop Grotteste College, Lincoln with permission

- good knowledge of the learner concerned

- secure understanding of learning objectives (for it is impossible to mark children's work unless both the child and the teacher are clear and totally understand what is the purpose of the lesson)

- knowledge of teaching point, safety skills etc. The teacher needs to be aware how they're explaining certain issues, what sort of resources they are using and whether the teaching style the right one for that lesson

- a structured approach so that the teacher can intervene and say *'well done that was a very good piece of work. I was pleased because you listened to the fact that the learning objective was capital letters and full stops and you've done that. But . . . 'you've forgotten to put various speech marks in your work, but I have to say' 'this is a distinct improvement on the last time you did this piece of work, you obviously understand and know more about capital letters'*

■ the use of effective and focused questioning of the learner

■ excellent listening skills — important because basically teachers will pick up key areas of understanding

■ clear settings of targets — this is obviously linked to the third bullet point. Teachers need to be clear on the number and the content of targets on which they are focusing.

**Planned observation of the learner** means that the teacher will have to plan and be aware of what it is that he or she is observing. This means that they need to know the learning objective set and be sure that the child knows it too.

**A clear understanding of the prior knowledge of the learner** — where they are in the National Curriculum, what they find difficult and what easy, will obviously help improve the quality of intervention when the time comes.

**Clarity and understanding of learning objectives** is crucial if the teacher is going to assess her charges and then move on to target setting. The teacher needs to understand what the child is doing and why. This is easier for the coordinator to arrange if the school has a clear teaching and learning policy which ensures that every lesson starts off with the reason why the children are doing the activities involved. For example, if we are about to attempt a piece of non-narrative work on '*The Vikings at Flamborough*' and the reason we're going to do it is that the teacher is going to find out if her pupils can find and present information from reference books, then this purpose has, of course, been shared with the pupils concerned.

Its important that the teacher knows the **teaching points and safety skills**. Does the lesson involve research skills? Are there any safety aspects that have to be dealt with?

The teacher needs a **structured approach** and an ability to be positive and communicate praise sincerely based on the aspects of the child's work. However, it is obvious from looking at the Flamborough story in this chapter that the child has made a number of errors and it's up to the teacher to make sure that a correction occurs which is explained clearly and communicated objectively and with good body language. Teachers need to be taught to look at the child, be open with him or her and then, in order to make sure that the child moves on in a positive fashion, make sure that your closing comments are positive and again communicated sincerely.

Questions often set the agenda. **The use of effective and focused questioning** of the learning by questioning the child can also indicate if the child has understood the main purpose of the lesson. **Excellent listening skills** are needed to benefit from the above. This will take time. Coordinators will however need to be sensitive to the problems teachers have with a class of 30+ children all wanting their attention at the same time. That's one of the main reasons why you can only set targets for three children at a time.

Some teachers find that just talking about **setting targets** will open up and identify the next way forward. Some teachers will write these targets in the back of their mark book or on the back of a page of work they are doing. Others find it more satisfactory having a target setting book which holds all these targets in one key area.

Here is an example of a teacher working with Sabhir and putting these intervention skills into practice:

❛ *That was a smashing piece of work, Sabhir. It shows real improvement from the last time we had a go at something like this last term. I liked the way you ordered the work and the way pictures worked with the text on the same page. You obviously have enjoyed what you've done. I was especially pleased by the fact that your handwriting really looks good now but I don't think that this part where you say that 'Flamborough is a lovely seaside town and has nice craft shops' would have been important to the Viking Raiders, do you? I think this bit shouldn't have been in here and perhaps we should have mentioned far more about how the Danish raiders came to the shores of Flamborough and perhaps you should have spent time explaining about their ships. On the whole I've been really pleased with this piece of work, Sabhir. You've shown good listening and I'm really pleased with the fact that our last target which was on handwriting has been achieved. Now if you redo this again and you finish it before half past three this afternoon I'm going to put it on that blank piece of wall up and there you'll get a house point. Well done.*

This example shows that there has been some understanding about what's gone on before. The teacher used a focus for future target setting and then set further targets particularly linked to time.

Where the demonstration falls down is that Sabhir doesn't get a chance to respond. This will not happen in the simulation exercise which you may set up with your staff. It may be a useful discussion point for staff meetings.

Getting teachers to improve their target-setting skills may be helped by discussion of the following list. Good target setting requires:

■ Clarity of objective (check against learning objectives)

■ The understanding of both long-term and short-term goals — dependence on the ability and understanding of the learner

■ The knowledge of where the stage of learning has reached — is this an introduction to a piece of work, is it practise or is it simply reinforcement of already existing skills that have been covered a fortnight ago?

■ The setting of challenging tasks based on knowledge of the learner

■ Clear communication regarding expectations

■ The inclusion of time targets

■ Sensitive and positive feedback to the learner

■ Children having a belief in themselves and their ability to improve (© Bishop Grotteste College, Lincoln, with permission)

High quality target setting skills need to be based upon what the child is trying to do and this is why **clarity of learning objectives** is central. Both the child and the teacher need to know why the lesson is taking place. What is the point of the next half hour's work on number? Why are we going to study the Viking landing in Yorkshire and on what aspect will we concentrate in the next lesson?

The teacher needs to set timed targets. Are the targets long-term goals or skills to be mastered by next week? For instance, by the end of the year do you want the child to be able to demonstrate Level 4 story writing or are you setting a short-term goal where, by the end of next week, the writer will understand and know how to handle speech marks? Time targets are vital. The best targets are those which include phrases such as 'before the holidays'; 'by next week'; 'next time you do this'; 'by this time next week' etc., the simple fact is that people (including children) work better when given time-frames. **Feedback has to be of a positive nature**: any success needs to be celebrated, although of course, also used as a way to set further targets.

**Is the lesson content relevant to the stage of learning?** Again, target setting may occur at the introduction of a lesson or during the development of a certain skill, for example, speech marks. Or it may just be constant practise in setting out the development of a story or the reinforcement of key spelling words.

The targets set need to challenge the child, so a **knowledge of pupil's prior attainment** is essential. The **Teacher's expectations need to be clearly communicated** in such a way that the child knows that the target is specific to them, is within their grasp and that help is available.

The pupil about whom the target has been set will have to believe in their ability to achieve it — or all the fancy planning; records; agreement trialling in the work will not work. Why, for example, does she believe that she is not using adjectives appropriately, or cannot subtract a two digit number from a three digit number correctly? Attribution theory has tried to explain how children's belief systems affect outcomes. For example:

 *If I think that my failure is due to lack of effort, I am crediting myself with the capability or resources to do better. If I think*

*that it is due to lack of ability, then I have no control, and try-*
*ing to understand will be a waste of time. And if I put it down*
*to luck, then I might as well carry on in the same old way,*
*waiting for my luck to change.* (Claxton, 1990, p. 134)

Thus for target setting to be successful, ideas (in both teachers and children) of fixed ability need to be changed. We all have to believe that prior attainment is not a limit to future attainment.

### Summary of the process of classroom target setting

■ Only target a maximum of three children over any period of time;

■ only set a maximum of three targets per child (these could be a mixture of academic and behavioural targets);

■ do not do this too often, base it on half termly impact;

■ the learning objectives must be clear to both children and teachers;

■ introduce pupils to their own target setting book;

■ remember not every target has to be written down.

Some schools have been successful by leaving decisions to the classteacher but school-wide target setting books for each child do give structure and importance to the process. The existence of target setting books can provide the same advantages that the assessment folders give. They provide a systematic structure that is followed by every teacher and is commonly understood.

The other advantage of a target setting book is that it allows teachers, pupils and their parents to regularly set and achieve targets and helps to define a culture of goal setting. In this way everyone is striving to improve.

## Using data to improve performance — a case study

In September the following bar chart was constructed by a Year 6 teacher after a timed story writing exercise, levelling the resultant work. Under test conditions she set the scene for the

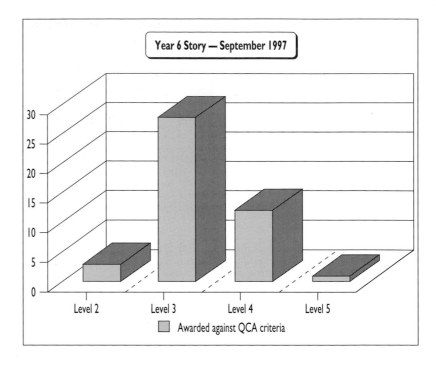

story 'The Open Box' giving pupils 15 minutes to plan and 45 minutes to complete the work. The story was then marked by a trained SAT marker and the levels put onto a data base. The results are shown in the bar chart.

There were a number of targets which occurred to staff when shown the chart and asked to review and explain the results. This was a matter for all the staff — all having contributed to the results obtained as the children had passed through all their classes. One target was set in five seconds — move the bars towards the right!

They targeted the following learning objectives to improve children's performance in En3 based upon this evidence. These included:

■ speech marks — all the children were required to practise opening stories with someone speaking;

■ how to write a scene such as 'on a beach'/'in a haunted house' in detail;

■ to try to include five lines on the weather in the leading paragraphs of stories and descriptions;

- targeting the use of conjunctions such as: so, and, but, because;

- setting aside time to focus on describing words such as adjectives and adverbs;

- getting children to concentrate on improving the beginning of stories in particular, as she knew from experience that the SAT marker would concentrate largely on the first page of writing. Hence she set homework such as 15 minute exercises to create a description of the setting or a story ending;

- she planned a multipurpose twist in the story which children could use in a variety of circumstances.

By target setting, using the criteria in the English mark scheme, she was able to tailor children's learning to those things which would increase the likelihood of children who were working at the level of a good 3 to produce work at Level 4.

She also became aware from the data that there was a significant problem with boys' story writing in particular. Apart from dealing with the boys writing in the same way as the girls by helping them to develop specific skills she got boys to cut down the number of characters allowed in any story to three. In this way she removed the tendency for boys to write stories which list the names of all their friends and very little else. This also had the consequence that there was a greater incidence of significant interaction between the characters (which is what Level 4 requires).

She allowed no violence of any description and no one was allowed to write about football matches. This meant that she stopped (the Level 2) 'Organisation of a story' which merely described a football match in which the writer's friends all took a star role. Boys now had to concentrate on writing stories with a set structure with more detail and a narrative. The teacher used her knowledge of the reference criteria for the Key Stage 2 SAT tests and her knowledge of the National Curriculum to improve the story writing performance of her children. After setting these learning goals for improvement

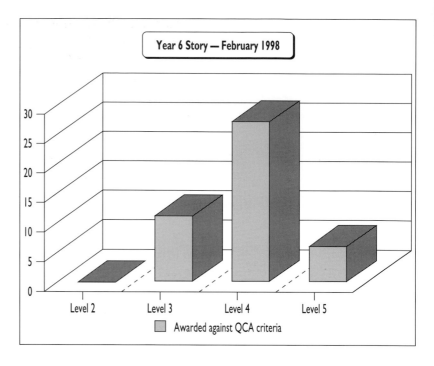

with individual children and working on them for six months the exercise was repeated in February of the next year. The same story was marked by the same marker with the same criteria.

The results are obvious. There is a considerable move to the right showing a distinct improvement in performance.

The teacher analysed the results further to show that there was a problem in the school's approach to creative writing:

■ too many of the children were working at a low Level 3 in story writing and the boys were frequently working at an even lower level;

■ insufficient time was being spent on the teaching of English skills — particularly comprehension;

■ set story writing skills, laid down in the National Curriculum needed to be taught in all year groups, and not just in Year 6;

■ higher order skills, those necessary to attain Level 5 were not being taught;

■ a number of teachers were still unfamiliar with the necessary features of a Level 4 story.

This is without a doubt an example of effective assessment of children's work and target setting. The end result was that *80 per cent* of children in that year obtained Level 4 SATs or above in English (compared to *50 per cent* in the previous year).

A number of schools use commercial Key Stage 2 diagnostic systems to analyse the test data in order to identify strengths and weaknesses such as those above. By the time the school gets the data and then enters it onto the database, the Year 6 children themselves will almost certainly have left the school. However the data itself is very useful. It can identify pupils' weaknesses in answering certain questions or even in their test techniques. In one school recently the staff worked out that in the science SAT the children's results in 'forces' were markedly worse than for other attainment targets. This led to a revision both of the way in which this aspect was taught and of the science scheme of work.

In another school the results in the later parts of the mathematics test were remarkably different to those at the beginning. (Indeed not one child scored on any item on either of the last two pages of test A or test B). The teachers were convinced that the children knew the content. The diagnostics showed them to be right — it was their slow exam technique which caused the problem. Children were unable to demonstrate what they knew because of lack of sufficient test practice. The teachers altered their plans and made time for children to practice timed tests. In 1998 the diagnostic analysis showed great improvement in the scores obtained on the later pages and as a consequence the school's results improved over two years from 23 per cent to nearly 60 per cent.

The compilation of the test results is extremely time consuming so beware in case it falls to you as assessment coordinator. It can be done by secretaries, headteachers, students employed for the purpose. If you work in an authority which offers to do this for you — even at a price — you would be wise to accept the offer.

| Diagnostic Chart — Expected responses for cohort — Whole school | | | |
|---|---|---|---|
| | Lee Giles | Correct items 21 of 40 | Unexpected responses: 2 |
| Least difficult | 1, 2, 7b(1), 10, 11b, 11a, 7a, 3, 6, ×13(1), 7b(2), 16 | x4(1), 8b, 8c, 14a | 5, 8a, 12a, 12b, 9a |
| Most difficult | ×15(1), ×18a, ×22a, ×15(2), ×13(2), 22b(1), 18(b), ×21, ×22(b) | ×4(2), ×19b, ×14b, ×20a, ×19a, ×20b | 9b, ×17b(2), ×17a, ×17b(1) |
| | number | handling data | shape / measures |

The process can be used to identify unexpected responses. This chart showed that Lee Giles scored 21 out of 40 and has two unexpected responses. This may not seem much but the boy was only one mark away from obtaining a Level 4. It will be seen that the chart will identify the least and most difficult questions. In the above case the reader can see that there were few questions amongst the most difficult that Lee handled well. This has implications for future teaching.

- Lee was assessed by TA as Level 4. Was he unlucky or was the TA merely a guess?

- Why were almost all of the harder questions to difficult for him? Was it the content, the style or the language?

- Were there attainment targets that were not sufficiently re-inforced. How often did the class work on data handling?

- Do Lee's class practise tests? Are they made to feel that doing well is important?

Bland numbers and charts do not tell you a lot. Statistics can tell you a great deal about the population but are of less use to the teacher faced with her particular class and her particular problems. The real use of data in Key Stage 2 is when it tells you something about the cohort of children who are with you for long enough for you to use the information to increase their levels of performances (see Figure 5.4). SIMS Assessment Manager, PULSE and QUEST are especially useful to schools whose LEAs use SIMS administrative packages. These packages can work together to save time and present data in ways the school is used to. The combination with other SIMS packages means that they can be linked to LEA central resources for data analysis. Quickly and effectively these programs will present charts of information such as those

| | 1999 | 2000 | 2001 | 2002 | 2003 |
|---|---|---|---|---|---|
| Cohort size | 35 | 37 | 34 | 37 | 39 |
| Target % | 60% | 70% | 75% | 75% | 80% |
| Target No | 21 | 26 | 25 | 28 | 31 |
| Pupils who should be secure level 4s by the End of Key stage 2 | Julie Sweet<br>Rafique Mul<br>Mary Wells<br>Fred Smythe<br>James Green<br>Freda Wells Ben<br>Robins Paula<br>Kay Karen Bird<br>Zanaib Nusret<br>Ismail Nurret<br>Luke Moore<br>Anne Smith<br>Alison Jones<br>Jack Kail (15) | Mohhamed Ali<br>Sarah Kelly<br>Rebecca Lewis<br>Amy McDonald<br>Jame McDonald<br>Martin Rowe<br>Leigh Jones<br>Tony Adams<br>Ruth Lewis<br>Jordan Clark<br>Ray Collins<br>Faith Cullan<br>Tony Beech<br>Katy Wight<br>Sarah Taylor<br>Jayne Edwards<br>Salik Raza<br>Dale Edson<br>Robert Ayay<br>Martyn Rook (20) | Kelley Tongue<br>Janine Brown<br>Maria Cassidy<br>Danielle Wight<br>Barbara Boyle<br>Amy Bayter<br>Jenifer Benson<br>Lindsey Burns<br>Leo McDonald<br>Carl Cantel<br>Sally O'Bear<br>Simon Sykes<br>David Cairnes<br>Richard Jaines<br>Ivan Harrison<br>Christine Lowe<br>Sahron Little<br>Stuart Horn<br>Ross Weight<br>Ali Khan<br>Shafaq Fenna<br>Wendy Burgess<br>Alan Duffin (23) | Jerry Terry<br>James Beam<br>Maria Caselet<br>Sid Danielle Ray<br>Barber Boss<br>Yamy Bayter<br>Jeniniy Benston<br>Lind Burnsy<br>Leovy Donald<br>Carty Shentel<br>Sale Rarer<br>Simon Syd<br>Davies Carley<br>Richard James<br>Ivovich Harrison<br>Sharon Lowe<br>Liss Ros<br>Dean Ross<br>Weight Ali Khan<br>Shafaq Fenna<br>Wendy Burgess<br>Francine Wells<br>Robin Benton<br>Ann Duffin (25) | Palmer, Owen<br>Brian Peters<br>Terry Moller<br>Harris Simms<br>Sykes, Meense<br>James Jennifer<br>Grayson Alexis<br>Rahel Patel<br>Mary Yeoman<br>Walker Jennis<br>Norris Hayfd<br>Masih Khan<br>Mark Finns<br>Thomas Jasson<br>Michael Kiha<br>Ron Usman<br>Simon Little<br>Ross Wintle<br>Fenna Shafaq<br>Ros Khan<br>Sara Duffin<br>Brian Wend<br>Stuart Horn<br>Collins Ray<br>Cullan, Faith<br>Tony Birch<br>Larry Burns (27) |
| Pupils who will need additional help to attain level 4 | Jamil Paisal<br>Wendy Hook<br>Jeremy walker<br>Joanna Wood<br>Mahmood Mo<br>Sarah Smyth (6) | Jenni Walker<br>Hayley Norris<br>Masih Khan<br>Jason Thomas<br>Mediha Usman<br>Fiona Mark (6) | Janet Grey<br>Justine Morris (2) | Ed Daleson<br>Alan Roberts<br>Rob Martins (3) | Christine Carrs<br>Ivan Jaines<br>Richard Harris<br>David Lowe (4) |
| Pupils who need additional support but are unlikely to reach level 4 | Lucy Appleyard<br>Jane Brock<br>Tanith Derby<br>Darren Wells<br>Scott Mount<br>Lee Brown<br>Sahron Janis<br>Tracy Gilbert<br>Connor Clarke<br>Ben Moorouse<br>Hussain Sharik<br>Kausar Malluck<br>Laura James<br>Ray Scholes (14) | Tamara Young<br>Kayleigh Morris<br>Mario Raza<br>Abbey Jones<br>Rachel Scott<br>James Rowe<br>Betheney Scott<br>Alan Edmonds<br>Matthew Rowe<br>Beverley Lines<br>Libby Unwin (11) | Owen Palmer<br>Peter Bulmer<br>Molly Taylor<br>Sarah Harris<br>Marie Sykes<br>Jennifer James<br>Alex Grayson<br>Rahel Patel<br>Martin Yeoman (9) | Kelly Saggis<br>Lewis Redcoat<br>Martin Leigh<br>Tony Jones<br>Rowe Adams<br>Ruth Jordan<br>Lewis Clark Tom<br>Walker, Hayley<br>Usman (9) | Lindsey Tongue<br>Barbara Brown<br>Maria Charles<br>Danielle Kelley<br>Walter Simon<br>Billy Bayter<br>Jennifer Leo<br>Benson Burns (8) |

FIG 5.4
Tracking cohorts through KS2

shown earlier. The package has the facility to identify, after entry of regular testing, those children who are secure Level twos and those who need extra support. This has important implications for target setting within the class.

It can be used by the head and classteacher to identify needs. It also brings into relief the moral dilemma whenever managers have to target limited resources and finite effort — just who should get the benefit? Schools have only so many books, set numbers of teachers, a limited supply of computers — there is only so much time. From the Target Setting Information Chart it is clear that this school will only reach the required targets if additional effort is centered on the children declared as '*Pupils who will need additional help to reach level 4*' and as this is both a national and local priority they will be encouraged so to do. The school's ambition to rise in published 'league tables', which registers the number of pupils reaching this threshold will confirm this approach. However this will, of course, be at the expense of teaching effort and resources which previously would have been expended on say, extending the capabilities of the brightest children, remediating the difficulties of those who have not made a good start to their learning careers, or teaching in the arts, sports, indeed in all non-tested areas of the curriculum. How many schools have now stopped running Saturday football teams, weekend outdoor activity holidays; how many chances are now missed to develop children's respect for the living world or for those less fortunate than themselves by organising charity events? The traditional variety of primary school activities allowed some children to excel, many of whom are never going to be leaders in academic studies. If we ignore children's personal development in favour of giving them a just narrow band of testable skills we have to ask if this is really what we want from our education system?

Nonetheless, by using the techniques and structures detailed in this chapter, the means to set and reach academic targets are now available. Those schools which have an ordered, whole-school assessment practice and then use this to set targets are likely to be the ones who succeed in this enterprise. Staff who have used these methods speak of a dramatic effect in raising the scores of their children, and this leads to greater confidence in both pupils and staff.

# Chapter 6

# Creating, maintaining and using portfolios of work

❝ *There is no absolute knowledge. And those who claim it,
whether they are scientists or dogmatists, open the door to
tragedy. All information is imperfect. We have to treat it with
humility. That is the human condition.* (J. Bronowski, 1973)

## Introduction

Portfolios of work are compiled and kept by schools in order to
achieve consistency and accuracy in their teacher assessment.
Few schools keep them for other than the core subjects of
mathematics, English and science, although work can be
moderated for all subjects. The background to this definition
of portfolios dates back to the position before Sir Ron Dearing
undertook his review of the National Curriculum in 1995.
Some schools had felt that they were expected to keep
evidence in every subject to support assessments on every
child. Some schools and teachers, under pressure from the end
of key stage assessment process, and the fact that it could be
externally audited, kept exemplar evidence for every child on
all subjects. The system was bureaucratic, unmanageable and
expensive. Dearing affirmed what most considered a common
sense position, that teachers should not be required to keep
evidence of every single piece of learning and nor should they
try. Whole-school portfolios of moderated work developed as

an attempt to keep the system manageable and relevant to teachers' and pupils' needs, as well as providing evidence for any external audit. This position was supported in the revised OFSTED (1994) handbook for the inspection of primary and nursery schools:

 *Teachers do not need to keep detailed records to support the assessments they make of each pupil: they need only collect samples of work which exemplify attainment at each level. Inspectors should use these samples to examine the comparability of individual teachers' judgments.* (p. 79)

Thus the school portfolio serves two main purposes. It provides evidence of standards of assessment within the school and it attempts to achieve consistency of assessment throughout the school and between schools.

*The Key Stage 1 School Assessment Folder* 1994 (SCAA, 1994) stated that:

 *A school portfolio containing recent work is the most efficient and manageable way for many schools to demonstrate the judgments they are making. They should illustrate standards in each core subject and the range of levels attained by children in this school. The school portfolio should include teachers' notes of empirical evidence as well as the children's written work. It should be annotated to give contextual background and to indicate the levels attained as well as the background justification for these judgments.*

Despite this useful guidance issues around portfolios are not fully resolved. What for example is meant by *recent*? Many schools have taken this to mean not more than five years old but unless interpretations change if the work showed Level 3 in 1992, why not now? You will have to lead your school in deciding what to keep, what to replace, what to update, in your portfolios of exemplar material. It is also necessary to decide whether the portfolio is going to be a year-group portfolio. If you are looking at Year 1 work there is no real reason to keep evidence of children's work beyond the levels normally achieved. The facility within the moderated portfolio for teachers to comment on children's levels is vital because it provides evidence and justification as to why teachers have matched certain pieces of work with levels given. There are numerous ways of using annotation sheets attached to samples of work and your teachers will be familiar with them.

School portfolios worked into the school's initiative on agreement trialling can lead the assessment coordinator through the process of developing and then monitoring the whole-school assessment policy.

The useful SCAA (1995a–c and 1997 a–g) publications which exemplify standards in each subject may be a good start for the school's agreement trialling. Although the examples given in the booklets are not within the contexts within which we are all used to working i.e. knowledge of the children about whom the assessments are being made, they do indicate the level criteria. A portfolio of the school's own work, however, means that teachers own the decisions made, know the children concerned and may be seen as forming a better reference point for future decisions — 'Is Sam's work up to that of Sally whom we judged to be level 3 last year?'

Portfolios are thus evidence of what teachers assess as demonstrating various levels of attainment in the three core subjects. They also have an important function in giving teachers an opportunity to test their judgments against those of other schools, wherever cluster groups of schools are able to meet together. One of the best forms of in-service is for teachers, when sufficiently confident, to compare their own levelled work with that of other schools. It can lead to a high level of cooperation over those areas where there is agreement and this leads to a further growth in confidence with assessment. As assessment coordinator, one of your strategies will be to arrange agreement and moderation meetings both within your own school and with other schools. Your close working with subject coordinators will be critical in the successful compilation of portfolios. They will bring the subject knowledge necessary to make your assessment portfolios accurate and consistent.

The SCAA Key Stage 2 assessment folder [1994] said:

> ❝ *The school may wish to keep a portfolio of assessed work which will provide teachers with a reference point when making judgments about children's achievements. It would demonstrate how judgments are made in their school and will reflect the standards agreed between teachers in that school.*

As you can see, portfolios will provide
- evidence of teaching and assessment standards,
- give the school secure reference points for its assessment,
- provide excellent training and development opportunities for all staff and
- be an important focus for any external audit of your school.
- Statutory requirements will be met.

The setting up and maintenance of portfolios provides opportunities for the assessment coordinator to monitor the assessment policy and to find out if systematic assessment is in fact not just going on but contributing significantly to teachers' planning and improving standards within the school. Creating and using a whole-school portfolio provides much needed staff support in making assessment judgments. The old truism that the more you do something the better at it you get it is well exemplified by the experience of most schools when creating, maintaining and using portfolios.

## What sort of portfolio?

Portfolios should contain evidence of children's work from every class but not necessarily every level in every class. Using this criteria it doesn't make any difference what type of portfolio the school adopts: a year-group portfolio, a key stage portfolio or one covering every two school years. Ideally the portfolio should contain evidence of two pieces of children's work for each level although in practice staff often find it difficult to confine themselves to this. What is important is that the range of work which would fit into any particular NC attainment level is demonstrated for staff reference. In practice staff find it easier and far more practical and useful to have three or four pieces of work showing the range acceptable within the 'best fit' criteria. Even now some teachers need reminding that each level covers two years of development for the average child.

As the portfolios are for all teachers they should be compiled by all teachers. This is an important decision that staff have to make, led by the assessment coordinator. In an ideal world all staff need to be involved in all decision-making but it is particularly pertinent with portfolios. Even if this is not possible, all staff must be given regular opportunities to make judgments about levelling children's work in the three core subjects.

As indicated, the portfolio should be limited to the three core subjects but include examples of ICT skills (from work in any subject). In practice, schools that have attempted to set up portfolios of assessed work for the non-core foundation subjects have frequently found that the portfolio becomes unmanageable, although clearly this is a decision for individual schools within the context of their own resources and priorities. It is probably best, certainly in the early stages, to encourage your team to be realistic and set a framework that revolves around English, mathematics and science. As a starting point and as a way of making the assessment coordinator's task more feasible during the initial setting up of a whole-school assessment policy, the following ideas can be considered:

## Suggestion

Coordinators, along with their headteacher/deputy headteacher, should formulate an action plan covering the next eighteen months. This will become the framework for compiling a portfolio, or indeed, the stripping away the old portfolio and setting up a new structure.

In **English** the portfolio needs to be completed for areas in Attainment Target 2, reading, and Attainment Target 3, writing;
in **mathematics** use it for Attainment Target 1 and Attainment Target 2, number;
in **science** Attainment Target 1 investigative work should be kept.

By limiting the focus in this way the process can be kept manageable and realistic.

| Example action plan | |
|---|---|
| Date | Action to be taken |
| September 2000 | Whole staff briefing on school portfolio — purpose and format |
| October 2000 | Whole staff agreement on portfolio structure and its organisation. Year portfolio set up. Year/School Portfolio set up |
| Christmas 2000 | Four pieces of work on one subject in each agreed portfolio. Two agreement trials taken place since September |
| January 2001 | Whole staff sharing staff meeting |
| April 2001 | Fifteen pieces of work in each portfolio |
| July 2001 | One core subject completed |
| September 2001 | Half staff in-service day. Assessment coordinator begins the process of a whole-school portfolio |
| Christmas 2001 | Two core subjects completed. Whole school review |

The purpose of the action plan is to provide teachers with targets within a framework. School staffs are under much pressure in a host of areas. Time is a scarce commodity and you as coordinator have to make your contribution to managing it realistically. Action plan frameworks help in this. If by April 2000 some portfolios have only say 12 pieces of work a significant start will have been made. Successful completion of tasks is critical to morale. Unrealistic targets, not achieved, demoralise everyone.

The simplest process for setting up a School Portfolio is to extract and photocopy examples of pieces of accurately levelled work and store them in a large file, with sections for each level in each attainment target. The format of the portfolio that a school adopts is entirely individual and will depend upon the size of the school and its nature. Schools with more than four or five teachers will not get the full benefit from whole-school portfolios simply because not all teachers will feel part of the process and certainly not all will be fully involved in its development. They would be better advised to put together year group or key stage portfolios. The decision will also depend on the structure of the school, but whatever the size, organisation and context, the bare minimum of a portfolio for each core subject for each key stage within the school needs to be set up. If a school has two classes in each year group then it will probably be most useful for the school to adopt a year portfolio. The obvious benefit is that teachers working closely together with each other in year groups will, when they plan, also use a certain amount of this time to prepare portfolios. This system simply gets staff involved. Alternatively, or building on from year group files, schools could also adopt the structure of a Key Stage 1 portfolio, lower Key Stage 2 portfolio, upper Key Stage 2 portfolio. Ultimately, the structure is less important than providing all staff with the opportunity to contribute on a regular basis. By contributing, their confidence and expertise will increase. If their confidence increases, their ability to construct quality portfolios will also increase as will their ability to set class targets (Chapter 5).

While the year-group or key stage structure is taking time to bed down the assessment coordinator can begin the task of establishing a whole-school portfolio. All that is necessary is for year portfolios or key stage portfolios to be borrowed, good examples copied and placed in what will become the school portfolio. Practical considerations, such as the size of the file, the use of dividers or plastic covers to keep examples in good condition and whether to include annotation sheets, will have to be made, as will the decision about how many copies there should be of portfolios, where they should be kept and how they can be accessed. One and a spare? One for each key stage? Consider manageability and the conservation of the world's woodlands! There are numerous other formats for portfolios. Some schools prefer 'level' portfolios. That is a portfolio for Level 1 maths, Level 1 English, Level 1 science. This is complemented by a portfolio for Level 4 maths, Level 4 English, Level 4 science. What we recommend is deliberately simple and easy to monitor in that schools should try to keep year portfolios moving gradually through to a whole-school portfolio.

Some schools have taken on the idea of children having their own portfolios as level example pieces of work come in. This is an excellent idea that shows progression and, providing it is done systematically across the school, it cannot fail to deliver quality practice. The benefits of children having their own school portfolios is very similar to the children having their own Records of Achievement, which are dealt with in the next

QCA describe their scheme of work in IT for Key Stages 1 and 2:

 *Any assessment of a formal nature is likely to take place towards the end of each unit; it provides an opportunity to review each child's progress. What each child is expected to learn is identified clearly within each unit as learning outcomes. Suggestions are also made about the use of presentations and displays. This will serve as a record of group progress, and the work presented could contribute towards a school portfolio'.*

(DfEE, 1998 p. 15)

chapter. Children who do have their own individual portfolio of levelled work find that it is very motivating. They have hands-on experience and can see where they are and can identify targets and, of course, see if those targets have been met.

The school portfolio could, for example, have a strong element of self-assessment, similar to the Records of Achievement in the selection of work. It would not be advisable to have both, as the next chapter indicates. But this individual school portfolio will be more teacher directed than RoA. It helps children to be self-critical. It also helps to set targets that can be achieved. Individual portfolios give the teacher a framework of reference for discussion with parents and with children and also can include governors. Individual portfolios help children to use a language they understand because it is 'real' work. The portfolio of work can make parents more aware of the school's ethos and philosophy. Individual portfolios also encourage children to strive for high quality and have higher expectations of themselves.

Individual subject coordinators need to be encouraged to be engaged directly and centrally in the development of their subject portfolios. More than one assessment coordinator has delegated the responsibility for the construction of the subject portfolio to the coordinator of the subject concerned. This will force them to consider (and eventually have to hand) examples of a good Level 3 piece of written work, or an example of a child just reaching Level 2 in their subject. That such portfolios exist will provide evidence to governors, students and inspectors on the school's standards and will mean that you are delegating to such coordinators real subject management and an important role in the public face of the school.

Having considered the definition, construction and use of whole-school exemplar portfolios of moderated children's' work, and introduced the notion of individual portfolios, we move in the next chapter to look in more detail at the recording of individual achievement.

## Chapter 7    Records of Achievement

 *Self-checking my English work helps me show off my best stories.*

(Andrew, aged 10)

## What is a Record of Achievement (RoA)?

The main differences between a child's 'individual portfolio of assessed work' and a 'Record of Achievement' are essentially matters of purpose and of scope. Schools frequently keep individual assessment portfolios in order to record pupil's progress in key areas of curriculum (often reading and number). In this way it forms a record of a child's progress through the statutory curriculum. It is part of the school's official accountability process, both to parents; the children themselves; and outside auditors, such as inspectors. A Record of Achievement, on the other hand, will probably be broader in scope and purpose. In whatever form it is kept, file or folder, pamphlet or book, it will include records and/or assessments of children's work, skills, abilities and personal qualities from both inside and outside the classroom. This will range beyond the statutory curriculum, impinging on areas such as attitudes, behaviour, interests and personal development.

RoA can be compiled by the child and the teacher or a classroom assistant. However, the crucial facet of RoA is that it concentrates on children's positive achievements. The record can be compiled, updated and added to at any time with the advice of the classteacher but it should all be within the control of the child. There may also be parental involvement. Parents can suggest and provide material, in collaboration with child and school, that they think might be part of the celebration of achievement in its broadest sense. An RoA is for celebrating success and sharing that success with all involved: the child and his or her home and school. It is thus a key to self-development which encourages the use of self-assessment as children engage with and make improvements in all aspects of their work and achievement. RoAs involve children of all ages coming to terms with assessing their work as well as setting their own targets and this is one of the most useful functions of the file.

 *The processes of self-assessment may . . . be clearly identified as integral and indeed fundamental components of the recording of achievement process.* (Nottingham County Council, 1994, p. 1)

## Parents' evening

This is an excellent link between home and school and should produce dialogue between child, school and parents. The children enjoy this activity (especially the morning after Parents' evening) because it proves to the child that their Mum or Dad have actually seen their work and have spent time commenting upon it.

RoA which help to inform children of the range of expectations of their classteachers will also be a means of showing them how well they are doing in relation to other children and it is of benefit for parents and teachers on open evenings. This letter was written just before a parents' evening.

 *Dear Mum,*

*Please look in my RoA folder at my work about the Egyptians. I did it in May 1998. I am very proud of this work because I have listened to the class teacher and she likes my pictures. It is my best piece of work because it shows that I have listened to the class teacher which was a term target that I put down on my self-assessment sheet. Do you think I have achieved it?*

*Signed*

*Harry*

Underneath there may well be provision for parents or grandparents to respond after they have seen the RoA:

*Dear Harry,*

*I like your work because you've listened to the teacher and all your words are spelt correctly. I am pleased that you showed me your piece of work. I think you deserve a Mars Bar when you get back home. Now perhaps you could try to improve your handwriting.*

The RoA should allow children to demonstrate both their achievements and their progress over time, by including a large number of pieces of work, certificates, reports, showing their success over perhaps five or six years. To do this they may choose to show off particular pieces of work and this helps children develop a critical faculty in that they will have to take work out and replace it by other work whenever they feel it is useful. Such a system helps children to appreciate current strengths and weaknesses because they will compare recent work with that done previously.

The technical term for this measurement against previous performance is *ipsative* assessment. Feedback from teachers, parents, governors, headteacher, will heighten the sense of celebrating and sharing the child's success. This involves the child in the development of important skills of self-assessment, that will increase their self-esteem and foster self-confidence.

## Contents of a Record of Achievement folder

There are, of course, many methods of keeping RoA, but a simple version is the easiest to administer. The format would be the same for every child in every class throughout the whole of the school. It is important that, given the celebratory purpose of the RoA, it should be kept well, with work well-presented and stored. Dog-eared or tatty documents hardly fit the bill. One such model is for each child to have their own two or four pin lever file containing plastic wallets each for one of the following features.

```
BIOGRAPHY
BOOK REVIEW
SELF-ASSESSMENT
MY BEST WORK
MY PROGRESS IN ENGLISH
MY PROGRESS IN MATHS
IT
AWARDS
HOUSE POINT BADGES/SILVER STAR AWARDS
LOG OF ACHIEVEMENT
```

## Personal biography

The biography is intended as an opportunity for pupils to show their class structure and includes name, age, address, telephone number, school name, class teacher's name, my special friends. This section gives a 'feel' for the RoA folder, making it more of a personal file that the child owns.

## Book reviews

Most schools encourage their pupils to write about the books they have read. Sometimes these records are then discarded but the RoA provides a structure for keeping them together and demonstrating progress in critical review. Children might talk about their books in groups in order to test out their ideas, and then commit their thoughts to paper covering the style of the book, what they enjoyed, their favourite character etc. Apart from being an excellent English activity, the reviews help children make decisions about their work and they are also encouraged to make value judgments about some of the reading material they encounter.

## My best work (in whatever subjects/areas are chosen)

This section provides an opportunity for children to make decisions regarding their best work in mathematics; design technology; on the football field or at the cub pack or whatever. They begin to decide for themselves what gives them the most pleasure, satisfaction, notion of excellence or quality. Over a period of time they review and revise their entries, refining and honing their self-critical faculties each academic year.

## Self-assessment

If this is structured into the RoA process, perhaps on a half termly basis, self-assessment sheets, similar to those shown in Figure 7.1, are a good way of getting young children to think about their overall work and in particular setting their own targets for improvement. It is important that children have a regular opportunity to take part in some form of self-assessment as the process is important in obtaining achieving a number of aims:

- Children need to have regular time to self-assess their own work and that of their peer group;
- Regular self-assessment leads to better target setting;
- Self-assessment by learners will help teachers make better conclusions relating to the actual learning taking place;
- Self-assessment can help to raise standards by placing the whole initiative into a structure;
- By going back to 'old targets', children are encouraged to regularly review and then make decisions about how well they think they are doing. (See Figure 7.1)

## Awards

The RoA could usefully be backed up by a number of other whole-school initiatives. For instance a house system where children are encouraged to demonstrate and share their successes. Certificates awarded and house points gained could be reflected in this way. One of the nice things about having a structured approach to RoA is that it allows the teacher and child the opportunity to keep and show off all their awards. Children can either place their awards into the file or take the original home and keep a photocopy. Allied to this could be a house RoA Board of Achievement where the success of all children in whatever areas of strengths they demonstrate, can be demonstrated, displayed and praised. There are of course obvious links here with the school's pastoral systems.

Name _____    Self-assessment Sheet

Date _____    Class _____    **My expectations**

| **My work** | ☺ | :\| | ☹ |
|---|---|---|---|
| My work was neat | | | |
| I was careful | | | |
| I tried hard | | | |
| I paid attention | | | |
| I worked hard | | | |

| **Myself and others** | ☺ | :\| | ☹ |
|---|---|---|---|
| I listened | | | |
| I cooperated with my group / partner | | | |
| I thought for myself | | | |
| I considered others | | | |
| I was able / willing to ask for help | | | |
| I shared with others | | | |

How well I did last half term

My aims for this term

© Falmer Press

FIG 7.1
Self-assessment sheet

## Implementing RoA

This is likely to be a further task for the assessment coordinator. The initial introduction of RoA will need to be costed. The price may seem excessive but once the initial cost has been estimated the future costs can be kept down to a minimum. The costs for the RoA file system mentioned in this book come to about £1.10 per child. That includes the file and the plastic covers and the cost of initial photocopying. The assessment coordinator may need to be at her most persuasive!

Like all initiatives, early planning is vital and whole-staff agreement on this subject needs to be obtained in order that everybody knows what they are doing and understands the importance of this approach. Any initiative needs to be costed properly and linked to the school development plan. If the assessment manager wishes to make life as easy as possible for classteachers they may provide all staff with their own reference file to make a class copy exactly the same as the children have. Teachers will then have a quick access to work. The teachers' file should also include information about how the system should run, the benefits of RoA and the same format that the teacher/pupil RoA books would take.

This section could conclude with problem-solving of this initiative (no initiative is problem free).

The main problems you will face in implementing and introducing RoA into the school are cost and time. How will the money be found? How will teachers' time be used and how and when this will actually take place in the classroom? Certainly it is true that an effective RoA system can be consuming of time and commitment so make sure both are there before an over-elaborate system is introduced. Again, the best maxim is probably, start small and grow gradually.

In summary, the three essential principles for RoA are:
1  the Record of Achievement should be ongoing, help communication, be easy to interpret and accessible to children, parents and teachers;
2  the process should be manageable for both child and teacher: again if its not manageable it will not be used;

3  the Record of Achievement should be used, for example on display boards and at parents' evenings as a way of involving parents more in the learning of their child.

Is it worth it? Some coordinators may be challenged as to the benefits of pupils having their own work files. Try these arguments:

1  It is very motivating for the child to have especially selected work in an 'important file'.
2  The portfolio clearly celebrates a child's achievement rather than failings.
3  There is a strong element of self-assessment in the self-selection of work.
4  Individual portfolios help children to be self-critical and also help them to set targets to be achieved. It acknowledges when such targets have been met.
5  It gives the teacher a framework of reference for discussion with parents, other staff, governors, children and it helps teachers to use language that children understand because it is for children — it's their 'real work'. Their portfolios contain a set of judgments.
6  Children do not always finish work and this is an ideal opportunity for them to have a system in place to which they can keep returning. It also can be used and shared with parents making them more aware of the school's ethos and philosophy and, finally, it encourages children to strive for high quality and have higher expectations of themselves.

# Chapter 8    Assessment and OFSTED re-inspection

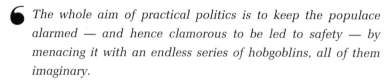

*The whole aim of practical politics is to keep the populace alarmed — and hence clamorous to be led to safety — by menacing it with an endless series of hobgoblins, all of them imaginary.*

(H. L. Mencken's wry observation in 1923 quoted in Morris, 1998)

In this book we have examined ways in which assessment coordinators could audit aspects of the quality of current teaching and learning and how good assessment practice can make improvements to your own school. Now we turn to external evaluation, particularly that undertaken by OFSTED. By understanding the processes involved coordinators will improve their own ability to examine the quality of their school's assessment practices and will be better prepared for the visit.

Although by now, all primary schools will have experienced their first OFSTED inspection, many individual teachers new to the profession will not. This chapter is intended to assist those of you preparing for such an inspection and to give you and your staff an indication of the increased expectations implicit in subsequent rounds of the inspection process.

Section 9 (now 10) of the Education (Schools) Act 1992 requires all maintained primary schools to be inspected by Her Majesty's Chief Inspector (HMCI), working from the Office for Standards in Education (OFSTED). The act specifies that over a four year cycle (now increased to six years) schools will be inspected in order to identify their strengths and weaknesses, so helping them to improve the quality of the education they provide for pupils and thereby raise the standards achieved.

---

**Key features of inspection**

All schools are inspected regularly;
- every inspection leads to a public report;
- inspections are conducted by independent inspectors;
- inspection contracts are won by competitive tendering;
- every team has one lay member;
- inspection is carried out to a published national framework;
- standards are judged by direct observation of teaching, scrutiny of work and discussions with staff, governors and children;
- parents are involved by being invited to pre-inspection meeting and sent a summary of the final report;
- quality control for the whole system is in the hands of an independent government department — OFSTED.

---

The inspection of your school will examine the achievements and progress made by children in both key stages, their attitudes, the quality of the teaching they receive, the management and leadership provided, the accommodation and resources, and the effectiveness of the use made of those resources, alongside issues of equal opportunities and special educational needs. Not all of the judgments made about each of these features will appear in the report but they will be submitted to OFSTED in the subject profile, which is the evidence base for the report.

Clearly coordinators are regarded by the OFSTED Framework as a key person with an overall responsibility for coordinating, monitoring and evaluating the school's provision. Inspectors will make judgments about the extent to which your leadership provides clear educational direction for the assessment undertaken by the school; the way teaching and curriculum developments are monitored and assessment is built into the process of evaluation and supported. They will consider:
- the way in which the school's overall aims, values and policies are reflected through pupils' work;

---

**What OFSTED really want to know**
Is pupils' work evaluated using clear criteria applied consistently across the curriculum?
            (See Chapter 6 Agreement trialling).
Are assessments systematically recorded and used to support learning?        (See Chapter 7)
Are internal assessments reviewed regularly?
Are the results of assessment used by teachers in their planning?
Do records contain a full picture of each pupil's achievements both academic and personal?
Are pupils using self-assessment to make improvements in their work?    (See Chapter 2)
Do parents receive regular reports and do they comment upon them?      (See Chapter 6)

- the way the school, through its development planning, identifies through assessment relevant priorities and targets;
- takes the necessary action to implement them and monitors its progress towards them;
- whether there is a positive ethos, which reflects the school's commitment to high achievement;
- an effective learning environment;
- good relationships and equality of opportunity for all pupils; and
- that all statutory requirements are met.

*The Framework for Inspection* (OFSTED, 1994) emphasises that a test of effective leadership and management is a commitment to monitoring and evaluating teaching and the curriculum and taking action to sustain and improve their quality. We may summarise these aspects of leadership as coordinating, monitoring and evaluating.

---

**Coordinating**
- developing an agreed view of what constitutes the school's assessment practice and its contribution to the effective implementation of the National Curriculum;
- identifying principles and procedures for interrelating the constituent parts of the curriculum in relation to the pupil's opportunity to develop their capability;
- setting out principles and procedures for using assessment information to inform curriculum decisions between and within classes;
- establishing the roles and responsibilities of all those involved in curriculum decision making involving assessment;
- organising the collection and distribution of assessment data to help achieve the aims of the school; provide coverage of the statutory curriculum; and, promote the educational achievement of pupils.

**Monitoring**
- monitoring teachers' assessment opportunities through planning to ensure that there is appropriate coverage of the Programmes of Study of the statutory curriculum and appropriate balance between different aspects of work;
- monitoring the assessment undertaken in classes to see how it has been planned and prepared and how it is actually carried out.

**Evaluating**
- evaluating the assessment of the whole curriculum and compliance with National Curriculum requirements;
- evaluation of the assessment techniques and organisational strategies employed by teachers, using the criterion of fitness for purpose;
- evaluating the standards and progress achieved by individuals and groups and looking for trends and patterns of achievement;
- evaluating the overall quality of the curriculum provided, including any extra-curricula activity.
- evaluating the standards of assessment across the school as a whole.

(adapted from Gadsby and Harrison, 1998)

---

The *Framework* is clear that it is the headteacher who is the educational leader responsible for the direction of the school's work and for its day to day management and organisation. In an effective school the headteacher has a direct concern for children's achievements and the sustained improvement in the quality of teaching and learning in all areas of the curriculum. Thus many of the above expectations will be **about the system of which you are a part rather than you personally**. However, all staff who are coordinators will have delegated leadership and management functions which form part of the above set of responsibilities and it is important to know those for which you are responsible and those in which you play a part alongside others (classteachers and senior managers for example).

What can an assessment coordinator do to make sure that the school's assessment practices appear in the best possible light and that if there are weaknesses the inspector charged with the responsibility for leading the team in their examination of the curriculum and assessment, fully understands that you are on top of them?

Firstly, you should try to make the time to look at assessment in the same way that OFSTED inspectors will. This is laid out in the subject profile which has to be completed by inspectors looking at the core subject, but in practice is a record of inspection evidence collected for all the National Curriculum subjects.

## The subject profile

Inspectors are required to construct a subject profile which summarises evidence and declares judgments about set criteria for each of the core subjects and also it is common practice for contractors to require this record of evidence for each of the other subjects inspected. The subject profile consists of the following sections:

- Attainment and progress
- Attitudes, behaviour and personal development
- Teaching
- The curriculum and assessment

> Standards are in line with national expectations at Key Stage 1 and rise above expectations at Key Stage 2. Pupils achieve appropriate levels for their abilities at Key Stage 1 whilst many achieve higher than expected for their ability at Key Stage 2.     (Extract from an OFSTED report)

- Pupil's spiritual, moral, social and cultural development
- Leadership and management
- Staffing accommodation and resources
- Efficiency

The profile is expanded below.

## Attainment and progress

Inspectors will seek evidence of the children's **attainment** in relation to either national averages or national expectations. They are required to evaluate and report on:

- attainment in **English, mathematics** and **science** by interpreting the results of National Curriculum tests and assessments to show: how high standards are; whether they are high enough, and any apparent trends in the school's performance. They use first hand evidence to form a view on the standards achieved by pupils toward the end of each key stage. Any differences between standards seen in classrooms and test results have to be explained by the inspector.
- attainment as far as possible in information technology and religious education using first hand evidence focusing on the achievements of the oldest pupils in the school;
- the strengths and weaknesses in pupils' current work in these subjects and their progress in them — that is, the effectiveness of learning in different classes or parts of the school, and among different groups of pupils;
- strengths and weaknesses in the non-core subjects of art, design and technology, history, geography, music and physical education (particularly swimming), using first hand evidence from sampling lessons and pupils' work as fully as possible.

(summary of OFSTED, 1998b)

The requirement to report on attainment at the end of key stages in the non-core subjects above is discontinued (IT is now regarded as 'core'). Progress will, however, continue to be judged where evidence allows. Thus coordinators will need to consider whether substantial proportions of pupils in Y2 and Y6 are able to demonstrate the levels of competence set out in the level descriptors for Levels 2 and 4 respectively. Is the degree of variation between pupils acceptable — has any variation to do with gender, ethnicity, age, classes to which they are assigned, access to equipment?

As a school can you identify aspects within strands of core subjects where children are achieving at Level 5? Do you know if there are some above these levels, what proportion are below? How can you show that they have reached these levels of competence? What records, wall displays, computer files of children's work have you got to show? Here your data from systematic assessment activities will pay off.

Advice on judging standards is available to both inspectors and coordinators in the SCAA booklets *Expectations in each subject at Key Stages 1 and 2*. Do your coordinators regularly use these booklets? Can you show that you do? Is your portfolio up to date? What about those subjects not collected in this way? When teachers have made those judgments about what individual children know and can do what becomes of the records? Do you routinely look to see how children's achievements increase as they pass through the school.? Do you as assessment coordinator give subject coordinators an overview of standards? Do you know how much progress children make between, say, Y4 and Y6? Is this *all* children, largely the boys, children with another language at home? This is where the assessment folder will come into its own.

Evidence of pupils **progress** may be considered in a number of ways:

- in lessons — where specific points have been taught do, children show learning gains? Have agreed individual targets been met? How often? Are they appropriate?
- over a year — as evidenced in books, files, and displays — are children clearly more capable than they were before?
- across the key stage — do children develop a range of skills, knowledge and understanding as they move through the classes? How quickly do pupils develop these skills?
- through the improvements shown by the results in NC tests.

Can you show that children make significant learning gains in any of these time frames? Can you demonstrate that children are making sufficient progress to ensure that national expectations will be met at the end of their key stages? Do you know? Does the headteacher? How about classteachers? Does the school maintain a standards book or do children have records of their own targets? (see Chapter 6).

Evidence of **progress in relation to prior attainment** will be sought in order to see whether pupils with special educational needs, for example, are being given the opportunity to demonstrate what they know and to make appropriate progress, sometimes through differentiated work or additional support. Some pupils who are particularly advanced in their work can be seen to continue to make additional progress when they supported in their need to have access to more advanced skills and techniques.

## Attitudes, behaviour and personal development

Here inspectors will be seeking evidence of pupils' attitudes to learning. Do you know this? Is this part of your assessment brief? Should it be? What is evident about the quality of the relationships between children when working together? What other personal development is related to the way in which classrooms are organised for assessment and children's learning? When considering attitudes, inspectors will observe the ways pupils approach their tasks. Do they demonstrate commitment to achievement, persevere and cooperate with others? Do children pose questions, attempt to solve problems and work collaboratively? Is concentration short-lived and a computer viewed as a toy rather than a tool? Can pupils articulate choices to use or not to use calculators, computers, numeracy aids to achieve certain ends? Do they use the opportunities for trial and experimentation systematically to improve their work or in a random fashion? Are children active participants in lessons, can they evaluate their own work according to their age and do they demonstrate a measure of responsibility for their own learning?

Inspectors will want to see whether children are being encouraged to use self-assessment as an indicator of how to make improvements. Records of Achievement (Chapter 7) are key to success in this area.

## Teaching

Evidence of strengths and weaknesses in the teaching throughout the school will be sought through direct observation and discussion and scrutiny of teachers' planning and records and examples of children's work. Coordinators who would like to 'inspect' their own schools might wish to consider the following dimensions of teaching:

| | |
|---|---|
| **Planning**: | How does each teacher decide what learning is appropriate at what times for which pupils? How does the work seen at the time of your observation relate to previous work, work in parallel classes, work in the rest of the school by older/younger pupils? Does planning take account of the National Curriculum; prior attainment by pupils; the work being undertaken by the rest of the class; and, or, the school's scheme of work? Are children given the opportunity to use familiar techniques in unfamiliar contexts? Is the planning appropriate for assessment to take place? Does the planning recognise that assessment has taken place before? (See Chapter 3) |
| **Aims**: | Do the learning aims suggest certain activities or are the tasks driven by a limited range of available activities? Are the expected learning outcomes appropriate for the age and abilities of the children? What previous knowledge, understanding, skills will children need to have in order to complete the tasks? Are the tasks differentiated to challenge different pupils? |
| **Assessment opportunities**: | Are opportunities created to determine the extent of the learning gained by individual pupils? How is this recorded? Are teachers helped to differentiate between different attainment groups by the results of previous assessment? Do teachers use different attainment types for differentiating the subject areas? Do they note the current context of the assessment? Are assessments used to inform subsequent planning? |
| **Pace**: | What rate of learning is evident? Do teachers press children by sensitive intervention and appropriate challenge to quickly move on to new skills and understandings? Are all opportunities used to allow children to develop their capability? Do children spend considerable time repeating familiar work or techniques? Are children given the chance to progress by being encouraged to suggest alternatives and extensions to their own work? |
| **Homework**: | Do children have homework based on their achievements in class? What use is made of the fact that many children will have access to computers and other IT equipment at home? Are children set tasks which involve research at home? Are parents part of the plan? |
| **Teachers' own knowledge**: | Are all teachers capable and confident in their own subject knowledge (TTA, 1998 a,b,c booklets may be of help here). Do they all understand the part they individually play in promoting children's development as they pass though the school? Can teachers use computers to create their own worksheets, label displays write reports? Are they all aware of the school's planned schemes of work? |
| **Organisation for learning**: | How are classes organised? How are records kept, are all available times used to maximise the use of teachers' and pupils' time? Do all pupils have the chance to take the lead in passing on knowledge to their peers? |

By considering these dimensions coordinators may be able to gain an insight into the way the quality of teaching, of which assessment is a main constituent, will be perceived by visiting inspectors.

## The curriculum and assessment

In this section inspectors are required to declare their judgments on the strengths and weaknesses in the curriculum and its planning and the procedures for, and accuracy of, the assessment of pupils' progress. Judgments about the quality and range of the curriculum are important for you in your role as assessment coordinator. Your knowledge and understanding of what goes on where, what follows from which aspects of capability, will be sought by the inspector.

Recently OFSTED (1998) has reported on the progress made by schools in implementing teacher assessment in the core subjects at Key Stage 2. This draws on evidence from HMI inspections and will be useful for coordinators who wish to 'inspect' the quality of their own assessment practices. The main findings conclude that in schools **where teacher assessment is used effectively to raise standards**:

- teachers decide how and when they will assess pupils' attainment at the same time as they plan work;
- teachers are proficient in using a range of assessment techniques in the classroom;
- manageable written recording systems are used alongside the sensible retention of evidence;
- teachers make accurate judgments about the standards of pupils' work based on reliable sources of evidence;
- there are effective arrangements for moderating teachers' judgments about pupils' work;
- there are effective procedures for reporting on pupils' progress and attainment.

In schools **where teacher assessment is unsatisfactory**:

- teachers fail to share the findings of assessment with pupils as a means to helping them to improve;
- records of attainment continue to be based on unmanageable tick lists;
- teachers' judgments are neither accurate nor secured through effective moderation arrangements;
- teachers lack confidence in assigning 'best fit' National Curriculum levels to each pupil;
- the links between planning, teaching and assessment are weak;

> The school benefits from an enthusiatic cocoordinator, who, with the support of the senior management team, has been able to enhance the confidence of other members of staff. The agreed policy statement and scheme of work developed by the cocoordinator strongly guides the work of teachers ensuring both continuity and progression.
>
> (Extract from OFSTED report)

■ pupil's reports are written on the basis of inadequate records.

(National Association of Educational Inspectors Advisors and Consultants, 1998)

## Pupils' spiritual, moral, social and cultural development

Inspectors will seek to determine the ways in which work across the curriculum contributes to the school's provision for pupils' spiritual, moral, social and cultural development. A carefully considered and monitored curriculum can enhance primary pupils' repertoire of learning skills; increase access to the curriculum for children with a variety of individual needs and from diverse cultural heritages. It has been argued (Brown, Barnfield and Stone, 1990) that group work can help schools to value cultural diversity explicitly and to encourage children to value themselves as part of human kind, which celebrates both similarities and differences. Group work can help to encourage children to look for strategies for resolving problems, especially conflicts and to capitalise on cooperative communalities. Using the Internet or CD-ROM encyclopaedias can help children to discover aspects of their own culture, particularly those which help them to locate themselves and used sensitively to foster empathy by imagining the feelings of people both in similar and different situations to their own.

How is the balance struck between the perceived benefits of the whole-class literacy and numeracy hours, now prescribed for the whole nation, and the need for children to relate to smaller groups of their peers, follow their own ideas and discuss matters which interest them? OFSTED's (1994b) *Primary Matters* claimed that a mixed economy of methods, approaches and systems was the most effective for a mixture of pupils with different needs, abilities and preferences. Does your school recognise this and bear pupils' spiritual moral, social and cultural development in mind?

## Leadership and management

The opening sections of this chapter lay out quite clearly the way in which the OFSTED framework requires inspectors to look at management and leadership, and assessment coordinators will be well advised to discuss their roles further with the headteacher to ensure that there is no misunderstanding and that time, if required for successful completion of the tasks, is allocated in advance. Inspectors will be likely to consider:

- how does the school's assessment policy fit in with the other documents available; does it reflect the school's values?
- is there consistency amongst staff as to the way assessment matters are approached?
- are all teachers clear about the contribution assessment can make to pupils' development?
- are there structures to determine if teachers need help and what support is provided for them?
- what time do you have to carry out your role?
- what financial structures are in place to ensure that the school can benefit from emerging technologies?
- how is the assessment system managed; how are decisions about new procedures made?

## Staffing accommodation and resources

In this part of the subject profile inspectors are required to summarise evidence and make judgments about the quantity and quality of staffing (both teaching and non-teaching), accommodation and resources. The effects on standards of any good or poor provision are critical features of this section.

It is usual for inspectors to be given a list of the qualifications of teachers and to enquire about additional courses undertaken, especially by the National Curriculum subject coordinators. Judgments will be made about the degree of competence of teachers in support of their teaching. Differences between the curriculum provided for different pupils because of their particular teacher's preferences or lack of training are not acceptable. The key questions for you to consider are:

- what are teachers' current competences?
- what are they expected to teach?
- what support can you provide to help them to teach it effectively?

Unsatisfactory provision and use of support staff may result in teachers' own time being used ineffectively, whereas the use of trained adult helpers has been shown to be effective in a number of situations.

As well as the courses attended by you, inspectors will examine the list of courses and INSET activity by your colleagues. Have you been able to arrange specific training for them — what has the effect of this been on the quality of assessment, the curriculum and children's achievements?

Accommodation issues include a discussion on the housing, storage and timetabling of scarce resources, lighting should be considered and ventilation will need to adequate.

## Efficiency

This is the summary of evidence and findings as to how efficiently and effectively the school's resources are managed and deployed. How are judgments made within the school to see whether finances made available to support teaching and learning are used in the most effective way? What do you or the senior managers in your school do to determine whether say the £500 spent last year on training, a colour printer or a set of NFER tests has been effective in promoting children's learning? Are future purchases based upon such information?

## Re-inspection issues

An important feature of re-inspection, as opposed to the first round which finished in 1998, is the emphasis on improvement. The threshold for expected (satisfactory) improvement is illustrated by the presence of all or most of the following features:

**Quality of education:**
- improved teaching in the areas where it was weakest;
- a successful effort to consider and redress areas of weakness identified in the previous report;
- effective action on the main Key Issues, particularly those related to standards;
- evidence that the school has monitored its progress.

**Standards achieved** — raw results

- schools with low attainment have narrowed the gap between them and average i.e. have improved more than the national average;
- schools with average attainment have kept pace with national trends;
- high attaining schools have sustained high standards;
- there are noticeable improvements in core subjects.

**Standards achieved** — in relation to similar schools

- schools which have had low performance approach the average;
- schools which did relatively well sustain that position.

Schools whose performance, despite some improvement, still remains below the great majority of schools are unlikely to merit the 'satisfactory' judgment. They will check whether.

- there is substantial improvement in attendance, attitudes and behaviour of pupils, if these were poor or unsatisfactory.

**Leadership and management**

- reported weaknesses have been overcome;
- resources and expertise being directed towards priorities related to raising standards;
- development of self evaluation.

**Ethos of the school**

- a staff-wide commitment to the achievement of high standards;
- pupil and parent satisfaction;
- good working relations across the school.

(OFSTED, 1998a)

The other change which can be expected is the increasing emphasis on literacy and numeracy and much of the data for judgments about this is collected before the inspection begins.

# Before the inspection

You will have between six years (if your school has recently been inspected) and two terms to prepare for your next inspection. Needless to say, that the most effective preparation for any inspection is to do your job as well as you can over a period of time (Gadsby and Harrison, 1998). Eventually, however, a registered inspector will contact your school to negotiate a date and sooner or later you will be told the size of the team and how many days the inspection will last. A typical urban primary school might have four or five inspectors over four to five days. One of the inspectors will be a 'lay' inspector, i.e. a person who has had no professional association with schools. Lay inspectors tend to spend less time in the school and frequently do not have responsibility for a curriculum area, however, they are full inspectors and will have an equal say in the formation of the corporate judgments upon which the report will be founded. Thus the team will be continually sharing evidence and the judgments they make before, during and after the inspection week. In terms of making judgments about assessment, this is most appropriate.

A typical deployment may look like this:

**Registered Inspector**: science; PE; attainment and progress; leadership and management; teaching.

**Team member 1**: mathematics; IT; D&T; geography; efficiency; staffing, accommodation and resources; attitudes and personal development.

**Team member 2**: English, music, art, history; curriculum and assessment, areas of learning for the under fives.

**Lay inspector**: pupils' spiritual, moral, social and cultural development; support guidance and pupils' welfare; attendance; partnership with parents and the community.

Readers will see that while inspector 2 will be responsible for completion of the school profile, evidence on the curriculum and assessment and write the appropriate paragraph, the evidence contained within it will need to be in agreement with the findings of the other inspectors who, while looking at assessment in other subjects, will contribute to the evidence base about assessment. Thus you can expect inspectors to collaborate and cooperate closely together. So clearly putting on a show for one week and for one inspector is not likely to be effective preparation.

In any case, every inspector has been trained as an inspector of literacy and will be expected to observe these lessons and feed his or her observations to the inspector taking a lead in this area. An additional day has now been made available to ensure that this area is covered in depth.

When the dates for the inspection have been arranged, the RgI will make his or her initial visit to the school which will usually involve a tour of the classrooms to meet with the staff. Although not officially part of the inspection, who can dismiss completely their first impressions? When you know this visit is about to take place you should make sure that the RgI is given the chance to observe what you want him or her to see! Largely this initial meeting is taken up with talking to the headteacher. The agenda used by one of the writers is reproduced below:

---

**Introductions**
The inspection team and contractor introductions.

- The school, staff, governors, issues and recent developments.
- Characteristics of the school, transfers in and out,
- SEN IEPs,
- Buildings, priorities, times of the school day, school roll etc.

**Procedures and methods of inspection**
- Before the inspection week — HT form, HT statement, curriculum documents, plans (layout), teachers' timetables, school visits/ extra-curricular etc. teachers' records, reports etc., preparation of children's books A, AA, AAA
- During the week — observations in classrooms, interviews with staff and governors, review of children's work and discussions with children, teachers' planning and record keeping.
- After the inspection — feedback to HT, SMT, governors, publishing the report, action plan.

**Agree future dates and arrangements for meetings/parents' questionnaire**
staff, and governors' meeting
parents' meeting
inspection team meeting

**Domestic arrangements**
room, lunches, services, payments

**Currently available documents/brochure/staff lists?**

**Any headteacher's issues**

---

Later meetings will be arranged to speak with the teaching staff, the governors and a further meeting with the headteacher is often arranged to clarify any outstanding issues, especially those thrown up by the statistical information provided by OFSTED to both the RgI and the school. The date for a meeting with parents will be set and arrangements made for a questionnaire to be distributed to parents. The questions are in standard form (see p. 164).

The following list of documents will be asked for:

- a statement from the headteacher and details as required on the head's form;
- the school's prospectus;
- school development plan;
- a copy of the governors' last annual report to parents;
- minutes of the governors' meetings for the past 12 months;
- staff handbook;
- curriculum plans, policies and guidelines or schemes of work, already in existence;
- other policy documents which are available in the school;
- a programme or timetable of the work of the school for the period of the inspection (deadline to be negotiated);
- other information the school wishes to be considered, such as school self-evaluation activities.

(OFSTED, 1994)

| Parents' questionnaire | | strongly agree | agree | neither | disagree | strongly disagree |
|---|---|---|---|---|---|---|
| 1 | I feel that the school encourages parents to play an active part in the life of the school | | | | | |
| 2 | I would find it easy to approach the school with problems or questions to do with my child(ren) | | | | | |
| 3 | The school handles complaints from parents well | | | | | |
| 4 | The school gives me a clear understanding of what is taught | | | | | |
| 5 | The school keeps me well informed about my child(ren)'s progress | | | | | |
| 6 | The school enables my children to achieve a good standard of work | | | | | |
| 7 | The school encourages children to get involved in more than just their daily lessons | | | | | |
| 8 | I am satisfied with the work my child(ren) is/are expected to do at home | | | | | |
| 9 | The school's values have a positive effect on my child(ren) | | | | | |
| 10 | The school achieves a high standard of good behaviour | | | | | |
| 11 | My child(ren) like(s) school | | | | | |

You should check well in advance (now?) that what you want to be said about assessment practices and the use of assessment data in your school is suitably recorded. For example, is assessment a priority in the current SDP (make it so); does it feature in the budget plan (put it in); do assessment related issues regularly appear on the agendas of staff meetings (put it on the next agenda); do governors take an interest in assessment and are such discussions featured in minutes (ask to address the next meeting); are there references to assessment in the documents relating to other curriculum areas? Documents which are likely to have most relevance to your role will be curriculum plans, policies and guidelines and schemes of work. You may also wish to check your teaching and learning policy and those for equal opportunities, SEN, and multi-cultural education. You are not restricted to the list of documents above, although OFSTED do restrict inspection teams from asking for more. If there are other documents such as assessment portfolios and assessment folders, which help to explain the work you are doing to support teaching and learning, make sure these are included.

Before the inspection the RgI will ask for the school and class timetables of teaching taking place in the week concerned to be made available and distributed to the inspection team. There is no need for schools to alter their normal work pattern but you will need to check these closely to determine just what assessment activities will be taking place during the inspection week. If nothing else you should know what is being done and how it relates to the school assessment schedule and if by chance very little is going on then you will need to be able to explain this and have examples available to demonstrate that the children are indeed assessed regularly and to some purpose.

Finally, the RgI will give the school, in advance of the inspection itself, a timetable for the discussions which will be likely to take place with individual members of staff and the arrangements for looking at children's work, current planning, pupils' records and reports, individual education plans and assessment documents. Make sure all coordinators are primed with the appropriate response to questions about assessment. You all need the same sheet. Why not produce a briefing sheet for each coordinator?

## The inspection week

When the team arrive in school they will almost certainly spend more than the required 60 per cent of time in direct observation of teaching and learning in classrooms. This will help them to confirm or deny their hypotheses formed on the basis of the pre-inspection evidence. As well as watching teachers teach they will

- discuss children's work with them in individual and group discussions;
- hear a sample of children read;
- scrutinise a sample of work from each year group;
- look at current plans and teachers' records;
- attend assemblies;
- watch the children at play and before and after school;
- sit with children at lunchtime;
- look at annual reports to parents;
- follow through individual education plans to see whether pupils are receiving the additional input and annual reviews they require;
- see whether teachers' plans match the reality;
- examine whether baseline assessments and National Curriculum test results are built upon in subsequent classes, and
- have individual discussions with staff, especially those with management responsibilities. This may mean you and if it doesn't why not ask for 15 minutes with the appropriate inspector? If you know what you are doing he/she will be able to tick all the right boxes after your conversation.

During the week each inspector is attempting to describe the standards achieved and the cause of those standards being as they are. The first priority is to assess and evaluate the school's outcomes i.e. what pupils achieve, in particular their attainment at the end of each key stage and the progress they are making. This provides the basis for considering why achievements are as they are, in particular, how effective teaching is, and how leadership and management impact on the quality of provision and what is achieved. OFSTED's *Improving the Efficiency and Effectiveness of Inspection* displays this diagrammatically.

| Educational standards achieved | Attitudes, behaviour and personal development | | **Attainment and progress** | Attendance | |
|---|---|---|---|---|---|
| Provision | Curriculum and assessment | Spiritual, moral, social and cultural development | **Teaching** | Support guidance and pupil's welfare | Partnership with parents and community |
| Management | Staffing accommodation and resources | | **Leadership** | Efficiency | |

Thus everything stems from what the children know, can do and understand, however, the inspectors will only be able to make the sort of judgments about pupils' attainment that you and the rest of your staff can. They do not have a magic wand. They will look at test results and the work provided, the displays on the walls and talk with children engaged in classwork and attempt to determine how close they are to achieving the national expectations at Year 2 and Year 6.

Every class teacher will be observed teaching at least one whole or part lesson of English and mathematics and the evaluation of teaching will focus on the effectiveness in raising standards of literacy and numeracy.

 *Some whole literacy hours and mathematics lessons where numeracy skills are taught must be seen; other literacy hours, English lessons and mathematics lessons should be sampled . . . and evidence of the pupils' literacy and numeracy skills and their application should be drawn from teaching in subjects across the curriculum.* (OFSTED, 1998b, p. 6)

Thus inspectors armed with such assistance will take their findings to the team and attempt to get the whole inspection team to agree on the final judgments about each aspect. Inspection week will end with feedback to key individuals and at this stage you will be made familiar with the main findings and the key issues that will appear in the report.

## When your report is published

If after the above process is over you can agree with Graham Dean (1996) that the inspection told us only what we know already, you will be well on the way to writing the action plan needed in response to the report. It will indeed be a replica of your school development plan and as such will cause you little additional work. Should some elements of your school's provision be found to be unsatisfactory you will wish to use this information to enhance your claim on the additional funds that will be at your school's disposal in the year following the inspection.

Recently, OFSTED (1998) has reported on the progress made by schools in implementing teacher assessment in the core subjects at Key Stage 2. This draws on evidence from HMI inspections. What you should do will depend upon the key issues identified. One of the most common findings is that assessment does not sufficiently inform future planning and teaching, if this or any other issues are assessment based you may start by re-reading some parts of this book!

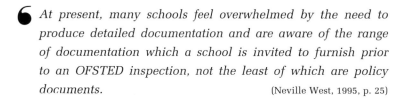

## Chapter 9 | Building whole-school policies for assessment

> *At present, many schools feel overwhelmed by the need to produce detailed documentation and are aware of the range of documentation which a school is invited to furnish prior to an OFSTED inspection, not the least of which are policy documents.*
>
> (Neville West, 1995, p. 25)

This chapter is intended to help you commit to paper those practices that you have been developing with staff, as described. Suggestions for inclusion are made for assessment, record keeping, making, and reporting whole-school policy documents and each is followed by an example currently being used in schools. However, for reasons made plain throughout the book, these are not intended as a blueprint for your own school, although you may use extracts from them if you wish.

Increasingly, successful schools have assessment features, which include: a written school policy; exemplar portfolios of pupils' work; individual records of children's achievement; and, assessment folders.

## An assessment policy

The school's assessment policy is the document that will provide the firm structure to bring the school together and thereby help staff to raise standards. A typical school's assessment policy could be presented as a number of sections under these headings and each is expanded below.

**Introduction**

a  The purpose of assessment

b  Statutory obligations

c  Pupils' entitlement

d  Planning for assessment

e  Assessment processes

f  Portfolios of levelled work

g  Background documentation

h  Review

## Introduction

The document should open with an introduction to the school's context and climate for readers who might include new staff, parents, governors, inspectors and advisers. The introduction should explain that the assessment policy is closely linked to other policies, such as those for record keeping, reporting and marking. They might need also to be made aware that the assessment policy reflects the views and opinions of the whole staff. The introduction will make it clear that school assessment will complement other school policies — importantly the equal opportunities policy — and be in line with the school's declared mission.

## The purpose of assessment

The policy needs to assert that assessment is the servant of the curriculum and not its master and that the school does not ignore or downplay certain subjects because they can't easily be assessed, and that you appreciate that assessment is an integral part of teaching and learning and serves a number of purposes.

These could be presented as follows:

**Formative** — assessment should inform planning for content and method; be used as an aid to planning and to mapping out the next steps in a child's learning; and for diagnostic assistance to provide a detailed picture at certain times in child's life at school, on certain issues relating to the core areas or core aspects of the curriculum.

**Summative** — that assessment provides a picture at a time of a child's development.

Assessment, you may wish to state, is vital in the identification of the way forward for the child, identifying his/her weaknesses and strengths. This policy may also be the place where assessment can be shown as central to the process of setting realistic learning targets for children.

## Statutory obligations

At the end of Key Stage 1 and Key Stage 2 teachers are required to make assessments about the levels achieved by pupils in the three core subjects. This should be stated in the policy. There are also standard assessments in the three core subjects which must be administered in accordance with instructions from QCA and the results recorded no later than two weeks before the end of the summer term. Pupils who move to another school during a key stage must take with them relevant teacher assessment levels for the three core subjects and other relevant attainment targets, plus other ongoing targets. Finally, teacher assessments have to be made throughout the two key stages although teachers are not required by statute to make assessments every year.

## Entitlement

These statutory requirements, however, are simply a minimum. Children are entitled to know where they are in relation to teachers', the school's and the nation's expectations. They are entitled to teachers' best efforts and hence for their teachers to know, through assessments in maths, English and science, how they can help them the most. On admission all children are entitled to an assessment using a baseline formulae in reading, spelling and numeracy. Junior children are entitled to a programme based on the known End of Key Stage 1 SAT results. Thus your policy might use this heading as an opportunity to stress that assessment is for the benefit of pupils rather than to satisfy government directives.

## Planning

The assessment policy should seek to ensure that over the course of the academic year the school maintains balance and breadth in its curriculum through its long-term, medium-term and short-term plans (see Chapter 3 on planning). For instance, it might be useful to stress that in the long-term plan the national attainment targets will be addressed; the medium-term plan, either termly or half termly, will identify the Programmes of Study and it will be stipulated that children will be assessed in all three core subjects. The short-term plan of the policy (weekly and daily) identifies the learning intentions, methods, opportunities and objectives that the staff wish to implement. This will include development skills and knowledge linked to the National Curriculum, and also will set out children's targets that will need to be identified and pushed on at a future stage. In this same section the policy could refer to your school's mission statement which drives curriculum planning.

## Process

This section is the reminder for teachers about what they agreed to do and when they agreed to do it. It might contain the results of various staff meetings or decisions of working groups. If your school is within an LEA which requires a certain assessment format then this should be stated here, but if you have a free hand this is the place to state what exactly it is that the teachers will be assessing.

For example:

 *In the non-core foundation subjects assessments should note any extraordinary talent or problem that comes to teachers' attention during the course of normal classroom work. Special tests or assessments will not be made.*

Or:

 *In English, maths and science, teacher assessment will be made each year against each of the agreed targets. A **minimum** of 3 assessments per core subject per term should be made. These will be aggregated to the level descriptors in summer term, prior to the children moving year groups.*

The example policy on pp. 175–7 indicates a 'best fit indicator'. If a teacher is familiar with the reference criteria and believes that on a 'best fit indicator' a child has achieved a certain level, whilst at the same time being pretty sure that he/she hasn't understood a certain element within that level descriptor — the level (grade) can now be given.

Ruth Sutton who has been influential in helping many teachers to develop assessment techniques, rationalises 'best fit' as follows:

 *Trying to get as close as we can to the reality of what a child knows or understands may involve techniques far more subtle and individualised than a multi-choice test. Talking with a child is more likely to produce evidence of real understanding than any amount of writing or ticks in boxes, but talking to an individual is hard to manage for any length of time in a busy classroom. If it is important to have an uninterrupted conversation, you may have to plan ahead quite specifically to allow it to happen.* (Sutton, 1991)

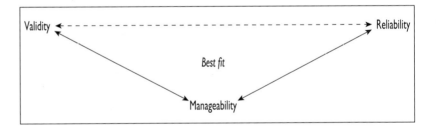

The policy document should also be clear in stating that teacher assessment has the same level of importance in the school as SAT results. This adds to the professional confidence of teachers. The equal status of teacher assessments is vital in establishing a practice that is systematic across every year group, every term. Teachers' opinions of a child's attainment in many situations, backed up by daily evidence, are just as likely to be accurate as a test taken one day with one set of questions, so should be seen as just as important as key stage SAT test results.

With teacher sickness, and teachers absent for professional development reasons, you need to be quite confident that part-time and supply teachers should be able to contribute to the assessment procedure. Such matters should be built into the process you adopt and and which are stated here.

The policy is place where the principles of good assessment practice are rehearsed. For instance, you might wish to state that children should be enabled to demonstrate what they know, rather than what they do not; that assessments should be carried out in the context of the classroom whenever possible and that they should be ongoing throughout the year and will be used to inform planning and teaching. Assessment should be rigorous and be shown to use a variety of techniques both formal and informal.

The policy should state that all staff will engage in the school's agreement trials. In some schools this means that every term the staff have one evening a week where they work together to make judgments about children's work. The policy will also be explicit about children's Records of Achievement folders, which give pupils regular opportunities to self-assess their own work.

## Portfolio

The policy should be clear about who is to be responsible for the upkeep of whole-school, key stage or year group portfolios and who should be involved in the process (see Chapter 7). The key to success is that all examples of work in the portfolios should be moderated at whole-staff or year group or key stage agreement trialling and that the school's policy on reporting or record keeping will be adhered to. To do this the SCAA Key Stage 1 and 2 assessment folders (1994) have proved invaluable. See Frost (1997) for reflective action planning and whole school audits that will enhance the process.

## Review

Any policy needs to have a section on how it will be reviewed, by whom and when. It is very important that these dates are written in so that effective development planning can be put in place. The following policy (Figure 9.1) is that currently agreed at Darton Primary School.

**Darton Primary School**

**Assessment policy**
**Date**: February 1998          **Prepared by**: Mr M. Wintle
**To be reviewed**: June 1999

### Whole-school assessment policy

## 1.    Introduction

1.1    Assessment complements and helps teaching and learning. It is an integral part of the National Curriculum statutory procedures.

1.2    This policy outlines the purpose, nature and management of assessment in our school.

1.3    The assessment policy is closely linked with the policies on record-keeping, reporting and marking.

1.4    The assessment policy reflects the consensus of opinion of the whole teaching staff and was discussed and agreed during the Spring Term 1998.

1.5    The implementation and ownership of this policy is the responsibility of *all* staff.

1.6    The school's assessment policy was approved by the curriculum committee and the governing body during the Summer Term 1998.

1.7    The school's Assessment Policy will, at all times, follow the equal opportunities policy.

## 2.    The purpose of assessment

2.1    Assessment is an integral part of teaching and learning and as such serves several purposes:
   - 'formative' i.e. that assessment should be an important part of curriculum;
   - planning and used in mapping out the next steps in children's learning;
   - 'diagnostic' i.e. that assessment provides a detailed picture;
   - 'summative' i.e. that assessment provides a 'picture' in time of a child's development.

2.2    Assessment is the servant of the curriculum and not its master.

2.3    Assessment is a vital part of teaching and learning and as such should aid teachers in planning work, identifying problems and helping children to make progress.

2.4    Effective assessment should lead to effective target setting.

## 3.    Statutory

3.1    At the end of each Key Stage (1 and 2) a teacher assessment (TA) must be made at the level achieved in each of the three core subjects of English, Maths and Science.

3.2    Standard testing in the three core subjects must be administered in accordance with the instructions from SCAA and results recorded no later than 2 weeks before the end of the Summer Term. At the end of Key Stage 2 the tests must be despatched for external marking.

3.3    Teacher assessments must be made (continuously) throughout the two key stages.

3.4    Pupils who move to another school during a key stage will take with them their latest TA levels for the three core subjects and their relevant attainment targets, plus any on-going targets.

**4.    Entitlement**

4.1    In addition to the statutory requirements, the following assessments will also be carried out in school:
- Teacher assessments will be carried out in English, Maths and Science in *all* Years.
- On admission, all children will be assessed using a baseline assessment or reading spelling and using SAT Key Stage 1 results.
- NFER testing will take place in all year groups, except Year 6, during the SAT week in May.

**5.    Planning**

5.1    Each member of staff should be familiar with the Programmes of Study.

5.2    Year/school planning for curriculum and assessment will help ensure breadth and balance. The three main areas of planning involve:
- Long-term planning (yearly). This allows for the national various attainment targets to be addressed.
- Medium-term planning (termly). Teachers produce termly plans identifying Programmes of Study and curriculum coverage. *Children will be assessed in all three core subjects.*
- Short-term planning (weekly and daily). The school's planning books will be used to identify the learning experience. This will include developing skills and knowledge, practical problem solving and creativity linked to the National Curriculum. Children's targets need to be identified at this stage.

5.3    The school's 'Mission Statement', agreed by all staff and governors, will be followed in all curriculum planning.

5.4    Planning books should identify the teaching style that will take place.

**6.    Process**

6.1    The Authority document for teacher assessment will be followed and used.

6.2    In English, Maths and Science, teacher assessment will be made each year against each of the agreed targets. A minimum of 3 assessments per core per term should be made. These will be aggregated to the level descriptors in the Summer Term prior to the children moving year groups.

6.3    Levels will not be reported upon in any of the foundation subjects.

6.4    In technology, history and geography, the teacher assessments should be made against the Programmes of Study.

6.5    In art, music and PE assessment is made using the end of key stage statements as a guide.

6.6    In all foundation subjects, assessments made will be used in future planning and be used as the basis for reporting to parents.

6.7    A child has achieved a particular level when the teacher is *reasonably sure* that the child could repeat the performance. A 'best fit' inidcator will be used.

6.8    Teacher assessment has the same importance as SAT levels.

6.9    Part-time teachers and supply teachers should contribute to the assessment procedure, but only the classteacher should 'log'.

6.10   Teacher assessments should:
- be ongoing throughout the year and often inform future teaching;
- be carried out in the context of the classroom;
- allow children to demonstrate what they know;
- allow for differentiated work; show a variety of assessment techniques and be both formal and informal in the approach;
- be rigorous in its application.

6.11   All staff should be familiar with the school's practice of agreement trialling and know and understand the requirements of the School Portfolio. The school will use the new Key Stage 2 additions of *Children's Work Assessed* published by SCAA when they are released.

6.12   All children should be encouraged to self-assess their own work.

**7.   Portfolio**

7.1   Every key stage should keep and update their own Portfolio.

7.2   Examples of work contained in the Portfolio will have been moderated at whole-school and year group agreement trialling.

7.3   The school's policy on reporting, record-keeping and marking will be adhered to.

**8.   Background documentation**

8.1   The following documents were consulted in the drawing up of this policy:
- OFSTED: *Handbook for the Inspection of Schools*, 1993
- DFE: *Circular 21/94, Assessing 7 to 11 Year Olds*
- Key Stage 1 Orders, 1994
- SCAA: *Key Stage 1 School Assessment Folder*, 1994
- SCAA: *Key Stage 2 School Assessment Folder*, 1994
- SCAA: *Planning the National Curriculum*, 1995
- Reflective action planning, 1997
- The whole-schoool audit, 1997

**9.   Review**

9.1   The effectiveness and usefulness of the assessment policy will by evaluated by all members of staff should the need arise, but no later than the Summer Term 1999.

9.2   The effectiveness of the policy will be the responsibility of the assessment manager.

FIG 9.1
Example of a whole-school assessment policy

# A policy on record keeping

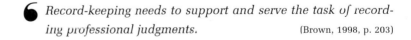

*Record-keeping needs to support and serve the task of record-ing professional judgments.*                (Brown, 1998, p. 203)

A policy on record keeping may usefully be divided into eight sections

1   Introduction
2   Reasons for record keeping
3   Statutory requirements
4   Entitlement
5   Portfolios

6  Special needs
7  Background documentation
8  Review

## Introduction

This section sets the context for keeping records in your school and includes links with other policies in this area such as assessment and reporting. It needs to state that the policy takes account of your school's equal opportunities policy; has support of the whole staff; and, reflects not only their ownership but also their views. The tone represented should be: 'Record keeping must be manageable and useful'.

## Reasons for record keeping

The policy should tell readers that your school's record keeping system is one that teachers can use easily to guide them to knowledge about their pupil's achievements. Again record systems should be used as a monitoring process that helps evaluate how well the curriculum reaches each child. You may wish to state that there are a number of records in the school which deal variously with:

- administrative matters such as who is on roll, addresses, next of kin;
- teaching records such as what has been taught, lesson plans etc.;
- learning records, for instance, who has mastered which topics and can read to a certain level;
- personal information including health problems, specific social skills etc.

## Statutory requirements

Teachers need to know just what they have to do by law and this is the place to present that information. This section would include the fact that some records have to be updated annually. If your school's handbook mentions assessment and record keeping then this same information needs to be written in the policy as well. If the governors have a statement on record keeping then this too should be recorded in the policy.

## Entitlement

Children are entitled to have records that follow them from school to school. Teachers too are entitled, on receiving a new pupil, to have useful information so that they can rapidly begin to meet his/her learning needs. When a Year 5 child comes to a new school and the only information to be passed on is the Key Stage 1 SAT results undertaken three years previously, a great deal of valuable time is lost. This is why we all need to update these records on a termly basis so that when a child leaves one school the records will follow him/her within the statutory fifteen working days and that they will contain useful recent information. Such records may consist of all SAT information, teacher assessments matched against the school's assessment policy, results of any internal testing such as the NFER reading tests, any valid information the headteacher and classteacher feels specific and of course any information regarding special needs.

## Portfolios

Portfolios are a very valuable part of the record keeping process. The school's record keeping policy might state that each year/ each key stage/ the whole school will keep portfolios in the core subjects. This will be for the dual purposes of ensuring regular experience for teachers in assessing children's work and the portfolios, that will have whole-school ownership, will be a reference point for individual teachers. The policy should also identify what it is that will be kept in the school portfolio. You may wish to keep information on reading and writing in English, maths (investigative work and number) and investigative work in science, plus any examples of information and communication technology. It may also say who will review pupils' progress on the record keeping policy and instigate the agreement trialling.

## Special needs

You should make it clear in this section that the special needs policy and the Code of Practice will be followed and complements this policy.

## Background documentation and references

Although not strictly necessary for internal school policies it is useful to know where the background information has come from for the development of this policy. Thus listing official publications and research data would give a professional and authoritative style to the document.

## Review

As with the assessment policy it is up to the assessment coordinator to date and review this report annually. This can be done in sections and should be carefully evaluated after the first year. Questionnaires might usefully be sent to governors and staff to assess their opinion on how the policy is working and the ways in which the form of record keeping adopted has helped teaching and learning for individuals.

The following record-keeping policy (Figure 9.2) has been compiled with the above in mind.

# A marking policy

The purpose of a making policy is to create a climate in which staff can feel comfortable, and a framework which they can use whenever they come to assess children's work by observation, discussion and perusal. Although good, coherent marking practice is your aim, the purpose of the policy is **not** to define exactly what teachers have to do. Each teacher will have practices that work and these can persist, even after staff discussion and be written as part of the school staff handbook. However the policy does need to set a clear framework which teachers can work to. The policy itself may best be divided into four headings:

Introduction
Purpose
Implementation
Review

## Record keeping

### 1. Introduction

1.1 Record keeping is an important part of our school's policy structure and is linked very closely with the policies on reporting and assessment.

1.2 The structure and process of record keeping has the full support of the whole staff and the policy reflects clear staff ownership.

1.3 The record keeping policy takes into account equal opportunities policy.

1.4 Record keeping should be **manageable** and useful.

1.5 The process should have as its aim the clear progrssion and cohesion of children's development.

### 2. Reasons for record keeping

2.1 The primary purpose of record keeping is to guide the teacher through children's attainments.

2.2 Record keeping is the servant of the curriculum in that is part of the monitoring process that helps to evaluate how well the curriculum 'reaches' each child. This information can then be fed back with curriculum planning and can be a useful part of the auditing process when a larger scale review is required.

### 3. Statutory Requirements

3.1 Records should be updated (annually) and completed tracking sheets passed up to the new year group teacher.

3.2 The school will follow the agreed significant logging sheet that identifies all teacher assessments in Maths, English and Science. A level of attainment will be given in each of these core subjects following the agreed pattern of assessment.

3.3 SAT results will be logged and identified on the school's tracking sheet by the classteacher. The headteacher will update the data base.

3.4 Parents have a statutory right to view records of their children.

3.5 The governing body has laid out a statement relating to records and is in the School Handbook for September 1998.

### 4. Entitlement

4.1 At the age of transfer or on moving to any new school, the Family Transfer Document will be followed.

4.2 Records should be sent to the receiving school within 15 working days.

4.3 Records should include:
- all SAT information;
- all TAs matched against the school's assessment policy;
- results of any internal testing, such as the school's NFER summer tests;
- any information that the headteacher and classteacher feels is valid;
- special needs information using the agreed family record.

### 5. Portfolios

5.1 A School Portfolio will be kept in all three core subjects.

5.2 To give teachers the regular experience of assessment, year portfolios will be kept first and later be built into a School Portfolio.

5.3 The Portfolio will indicate the school's vision and practice on assessment.

5.4 The format of the School Portfolio has whole staff ownership and will include:
- examples of evidence from Maths, English and Science;
- two pieces of evidence from each level on every Attainment Target;
- work will be labelled and background and content indicated;
- only examples of work from the following areas will be recorded
    En 2/3
    Ma 1/2
    Sc 1
    IT.

5.5 All teachers will be responsible in following the school's Action Plan in compiling the School Portfolio.

5.6 The assessment manager is responsible for reviewing progress and instigating agreement trialling.

5.7 The year/School Portfolio will be reviewed when necessary, but at least annually (see Point 8).

**6. Special needs**

6.1 The school's policy on special needs and the Code of Practice will be followed.

**7. Background documentation**

- DFE Circular 11/93 National Curriculum
- SCAA Key Stage 1 School Assessment Folder, 1994
- SCAA Key Stage 2 School Assessment Folder, 1994

**8. Review**

8.1 The assessment manager will review the policy annually, but no later than (July) 1999.

8.2 A structured questionnaire will be used to assess staff opinion after one year.

8.3 All governors will be kept informed through the curriculum committee and then through a full governing body meeting.

8.4 The school's Action Plan will be followed.

FIG 9.2
Example of a record keeping policy

## Introduction

The marking policy (Figure 9.3, p. 184) is integral to the policies of assessment, record keeping and reporting. Marking is an important aspect of the assessment process and where marking is seen as positive this is in line with the school's endeavour to encourage pupils' self-assessment. This meets with the school's policies on raising standards, is in line with the school's high expectations. The marking policy will always take into account the school's equal opportunities policy.

**Suggestion**

Work out with yor colleagues how you each ensure that children take note of the teachers' comments and that you all mark for content — not just style and presentation.

## Purpose

Marking is an essential part of the teaching and learning process and as such is an important way of feeding back to children their teacher's satisfaction and expectations. Marking is one way of informing the child if they've succeeded in achieving the lesson's learning objective. It's a useful way of keeping the child focused on agreed targets and there is no doubt that effective marking provides a path through which the child can make sense of his or her world inside the classroom.

## Implementation

How do schools actually implement a system that is systematic, yet preserve teachers' rights to do it in their own way? For instance should you say

 *most children's work will be marked in red and whenever possible with the child concerned?*

We have good reason for stating this, in that many children expect red marking and it is easier to pick out because they don't write in red. But you may consider this as unworthy of such debate if any teachers object. More important is to try to establish that teachers should mark with children and the most effective form of marking is to have the child sitting next you. You should also try to gain agreement that the most effective form of marking is one which is given back quickly. Your school policy on marking should be clear that all teachers need to maximise their intervention skills.

## Implementation

This section of the marking policy should show that the school and the governing body see self-assessment as crucial to raising standards. Self-assessment is an important feature in encouraging children to expect more of themselves.

An unfortunate feature of school life is that some supply teachers do not always mark the work they have undertken with their classes. Your policy should say what the responsibility of such relief teachers should be and then show them this policy when they come into school. It is as well to

## Policy for Marking

**Darton Primary School**
**Prepared by**: M. Wintle/S. Economou    **Date**: May 1997
**To be reviewed**: Autumn Term 1998

### 1.    Introduction

1.1    The marking policy belongs with the set of policies on assessment, record keeping and reporting.

1.2    Marking is an important part of assessment.

1.3    Through this policy, it is hoped to encourage the child to look at errors in a positive manner. This is in line with the school's positive approach on self-assessment.

1.4    The marking policy takes into account the school's policy on equal opportunities.

### 2.    Purpose

2.1    Marking is an essential part of the learning process and as such is one important way of informing children of teacher satisfaction and expectations.

2.2    Marking is an effective way of keeping the child focused on agreed targets.

2.3    Marking can be the 'path' through which a child makes sense of the curriculum.

### 3.    Implementation

3.1    Most work should be marked mostly in red pen and whenever possible with the child concerned.

3.2    Marking should be handed back quickly to encourage discussion of the work.

3.3    The teacher's professional judgment is the key factor in all assessment. Therefore, marking is often judgmental and selective in order to foster positive attitudes in our children.

3.4    Our children should be encouraged to mark their own/group work. Self-assessment has an important role in the school's practice in RoA.

3.5    Relief teachers should mark all set work and return it to class teachers. (For Aurumn Term 1997)

3.6    House points are awarded for good work and the basis for these is as follows:
- HPs are awarded for work done in and outside the classrooms.
- HPs are seen as a completion of targets.
- A maximum of 3 HPs are awarded for one piece of work.
- The children are clear in their understanding of the House Points System.
- HPs can be awarded for good deeds.
- Badges are encouraged and seen as a sign of achievement.

3.7    Teacher comments should be mainly positive and always legible.

3.8    Comments should be written in the appropriate language for the individual child's age and ability.

3.9    Quality work can be kept in the child's RoA wallet.

3.10    Teachers should mainly write positive comments inside a cloud and targets within a box.

### 4.    Review

4.1    This marking policy will be reviewed in the Autumn Term 1998, or when the need arises.

4.2    The policy is the responsibility of the assessment coordinator.

FIG 9.3
An example of a marking policy

state the obvious, that when teachers do mark the comments they make should be positive and legible and that the language used should be capable of being understood easily by the children. The policy should also detail how marking should relate to any house point system adopted by your school.

The marking policy shown below links to the record of achievement system and refers to boxes and clouds. This means that when a teacher writes a positive comment for example, '*well done, Mary, you've listened to the purpose of the lesson of writing a first draft piece of work in a logical order*', if that's a positive comment or even 'well done' these comments are put in a cloud. If there are targets to be set such as, '*you haven't put down . . . you have forgotten that 100 pence make a pound, or 10 millimetres are in 1 centimetre and by next Wednesday I want you to have learned that*', these targets, even word corrections, are put within a box.

### Review

The policy, Figure 9.3, is dated and a review date stated.

## A policy for reporting to parents/guardians

The policy needs to be shown to be linked to those of assessment and record keeping and to state timing of its inception and links to the equal opportunity policy.

Reports are of limited value to parents if they just consist of the detail of the National Curriculum content pupils have covered during the last year. Open evenings, newsletters etc. can cover this ground and parents who are involved in the target setting process will have been given even more detail about the intended curriculum. In the report, parents expect teachers to make professional judgments about their children's attainment and progress and be clear about any problems they may have. Parents have a right to be informed about the relative achievements of their children and detailed, truthful reports are an important element in the home/school partnership.

In particular, schools need to report to parents how well their children are doing in the core and foundation subjects. Some successful schools, in an effort to eliminate course content from reports, have produced in September 'Information for Parents' booklets which serve two purposes:

■ They inform parents of the year's curriculum content that their children will be meeting.
■ They take away this aspect from report writing.

It is interesting that on reviewing hundreds of parental questionnaires that there is still concern relating to computer-generated reports. On the whole teachers prefer computerised reports. A professional report can be produced in a fraction of the time. On the other hand, parents still view computer-generated reports with suspicion and, on the whole, seem to prefer the hand written versions, perhaps because they are precieved to be more personal. Such choices should be be discussed by the whole staff, but the assessment coordinator may wish to instigate such a discussion. The policy statement given as an example at the end of this section (Figure 9.4) relates to hand written reports.

A number of more mundane (but still important) policy statements are included here for you and your colleagues to consider. Presentation is important. We expect good presentational skills in our pupils, so we ourselves should set a good example.

■ Good quality paper will be used and teachers' writing needs to be legible and neat. This creates a good professional impression.
■ Black pen will be used. This is a help when reports are photocopied for individual records as part of the child's development picture.
■ Important assessment data such as reading ages or standardised test results need to be entered onto the report and, if necessary, explained by the classteacher during the following parents' evening. This is an obvious area of teacher concern but parents have a right to know.
■ Schools need to be aware of the circumstances in their children's homes. Are large print reports for partially sighted parents available, and the point 4.10 is especially relevant in today's age of legality.
■ Head teachers need to be aware that parents have a right to view all their child's records.

## A reporting policy

### 1. Introduction

1.1 Reporting is an important part of the school's policy on assessment. Therefore, this policy is closely linked with the policies on assessment and record keeping.

1.2 The structure and process of reporting to parents has the full support of the staff and governors and was drawn up during the Autumn Term 1998.

1.3 The reporting policy should take into account the equal opportunities policy and be especially aware of the needs of all our parents.

1.4 The written report should be useful to parents in showing the development of their children within the framework of the National Curriculum.

### 2. Reasons for reporting

2.1 The primary purpose of reporting is to guide the parent/guardian regarding the child's progress.

2.2 The key contents of the report will cover the three core elements of the National Curriculum.

### 3. Statutory requirements

3.1 Parents will receive the report every year (July in all cases).

3.2 Parents will receive the opportunity to comment on their child's report.

3.3 SAT levels will be given out in Year 2 and Year 6. Comparisons will be made with national statistics.

3.4 The governing body has laid out a statement on reporting and it is contained in the School Handbook for September 1999.

### 4. Implementation

4.1 All reports will be written on good quality paper. Reports should be legible and contain no examples of correction. Black pen is to be used at all times.

4.2 Reports will go out to parents in July and be backed up by returned comments slips and a full Parents' Evening. These will occur within two weeks of parents receiving the report.

4.3 All reports will detail progress and comment on strengths and weaknesses of the child. This is the fundamental requirement of our report writing.

4.4 Reporting to parents should be linked to the September issue of the booklets 'Information to Parents'.

4.5 Any annual data will be included in the report and this should include reading ages, Maths Standardised Scores (SS) and any special needs reporting.

4.6 Maths setting will mean the child's Maths teacher will complete their Maths groups subject reports.

4.7 All reports should be given to the head teacher one week before their issue. This is in order for the head to check and comment on each report.

4.8 Any special needs staging will be referred to and IEPs should be brought to the attention of the parent/guardian.

4.9 Unless in specific circumstances, separated parents can each be issued with a copy of their child's report.

4.10 Copies of each report will be stored in each child's record card and kept in the head teacher's office. Parents have a right to view all records.

**5.    Background documentation**

5.1 Parents' questionnaire of July, 1998.

**6.    Review**

6.1 The assessment manager will review the reporting policy in the Autumn Term 1999.

6.2 All governors will be kept fully informed through the curriculum committee and then through a full governing body meeting.

6.3 The school's Development Plan will be followed at all times.

FIG 9.4
Example of a reporting policy

# Bibliography

BASTIDE, D. (1998) *Coordinating religious education across the primary school*, London: Falmer Press.

BELBIN, R. M. (1981) *Management Teams: Why they succeed or fail*, Oxford: Butterworth–Heinemann.

BIRCH, J. (1995) 'Coordinating English at Key Stage 1' in DAVIES, J. (ed) *Developing a Leadership Role in the Key Stage 1 Curriculum*, London: Falmer Press.

BIRCH, T. (1995) 'Developing the role of the Key Stage 1 IT coordinator: A case of the hare or the tortoise' in DAVIES, J. (ed) *Developing a Leadership Role in the Key Stage 1 Curriculum*, London: Falmer Press.

BLACK, P. (1998) *Testing: Friend Or Foe? Theory and Practice of Assessment and Testing*, London: Falmer Press.

BLEASE, D. and LEVER, D. (1992) 'What do primary headteachers really do?', *Educational Studies*, **8**, 2.

BOEKESTEIN, D. (1995) 'Tackling technology in the early years' in DAVIES, J. (ed) *Developing a Leadership Role in the Key Stage 1 Curriculum*, London: Falmer Press.

BOWE, K. (1995) 'The new science coordinator' in DAVIES, J. (ed) *Developing a Leadership Role in the Key Stage 1 Curriculum*, London: Falmer Press.

BOYLE, B. (1995) 'Providing a sense of direction in Key Stage 2' in HARRISON, M. (ed) *Developing a Leadership Role in the Key Stage 2 Curriculum*, London: Falmer Press.

BRONOWSKI, J. (1973) *The Ascent of Man*, London: BBC.

BROWN, C., BARNFIELD, J. and STONE, M. (1990) *A Spanner in the Works: Primary School Teaching for Equality and Justice*, Stoke-on-Trent: Trentham Books.

BROWN, T. (1998) *Coordinating mathematics across the primary school*, London: Falmer Press.

CAMPBELL, J., EVANS, L., NEILL, S. and PACKWOOD, A. (1993) 'The National Curriculum and the management of infant teachers' time' in PREEDY, M. (ed) *Managing the Effective School*, London: PCP.

CAMPBELL, J. and NEILL, S. R. (1994) *Primary Teachers at Work*, London: Routledge.

CHEDZOY, S. (1995) 'Developing a leadership role at Key Stage 1 — physical education' in DAVIES, J. (ed) *Developing a Leadership Role in the Key Stage 1 Curriculum*, London: Falmer Press.

CHURCHILL, W. L. S. (1985) quoted in 'It's not a test for the best' by John Matthews in the *Daily Telegraph*, 3.9.85.

CLAXTON, G. (1990) *Teaching to Learn*, London: Cassell.

CLEMENT, R., PIOTROWSKI, J. and ROBERTS, I. (1998) *Coordinating art across the primary school*, London: Falmer Press.

CLEMSON, D. and CLEMSON, W. (1996) *The Really Practical Guide to Primary Assessment*, Cheltenham: Stanley Thornes.

COVEY, S. R. (1992) *Seven Habits of Highly Effective People*, London: Schuster and Schuster.

CROLL, P. and MOSES, D. (1985) *One in Five, the Assessment and Incidence of Special Educational Needs*, London: RKP.

CROSS, A. (1995) 'Design and Technology at Key Stage 2' in HARRISON, M. (ed) *Developing a Leadership Role in the Key Stage 2 Curriculum*, London: Falmer Press.

CROSS, A. (1998) *Coordinating design and technology across the primary school*, London: Falmer Press.

CROSS, A. and BYRNE, D. (1995) 'Coordinating science at Key Stage 2' in HARRISON, M. (ed) *Developing a Leadership Role in the Key Stage 2 Curriculum*, London: Falmer Press.

CROSS, A. and CROSS, S. (1993) 'Running a professional development day in your school' in HARRISON, M. (ed) *Beyond the Core Curriculum*, Plymouth: Northcote House.

DAVIES, J. (1995) 'The history coordinator at Key Stage 1' in
    DAVIES, J. (ed) *Developing a Leadership Role in the Key Stage 1
    Curriculum*, London: Falmer Press.

DAVIES, J. (1995a) 'The history coordinator in Key Stage 2' in
    HARRISON, M. (ed) *Developing a Leadership Role in the Key
    Stage 2 Curriculum*, London: Falmer Press.

DAVIES, J. and REDMOND, J. (1998) *Coordinating history across the
    primary school*, London: Falmer Press.

DEAN, G. (1996) 'Inspecting IT', *Interactive December 1996*, pp. 17–19.

DEAN, J. (1987) *Managing the Primary School*, Kent, Croome Helm.

DES (1978) *Primary Education in England*, London: HMSO.

DES (1987) *TGAT Report*, London: HMSO.

DES (1991) *Interim Advisory Committee on School Teachers' Pay and
    Conditions, Fourth report*, London: HMSO.

DES (1991a) *Developing School Management: Report by the School
    Management Task Force*, London: HMSO.

DFE (1994) *The National Curriculum and its Assessment: Final
    Report (The Dearing Report)*, London: HMSO.

DfEE (1997) *From Targets into Action: Guidance to Support Effective
    Target-setting in Schools*, London: HMSO.

DfEE (1998) *Information Technology: Teacher's Guide*, London: QCA.

DfEE/QCA (1998a) *1997 Benchmarking Information for Key Stages 1
    and 2*, London: QCA.

DfEE/QCA (1998b) *The National Literacy Strategy*, London: QCA.

DIXON, A. (1997) 'Play it again, Sam — Streaming revisited', *Forum*,
    **39**, 3.

EASEN, P. (1989) *Making School INSET Work*, London: OU Press.

EDWARDS, A. (1993) 'Curriculum coordination: a lost opportunity for
    primary schools', *School Organisation*, **13**, 1, pp. 51–9.

EVERARD, K. B. and MORRIS, G. (1985) *Effective School
    Management*, London: PCP.

FROST, D. (1997) *Reflective Action Planning for Teachers*, London:
    David Fulton.

GADSBY, P. and HARRISON, M. (1998) *OFSTED re-inspection and
    the primary coordinator*, London: Falmer Press.

GALTON, M. (1995) *Crisis in the Primary Classroom*, London: David Fulton.

GHOURT, N. (1998) 'Tests brand boys as failures', *TES* 19.6.98.

GOOD, T. L. and BROPHY, J. E. (1991) *Looking in Classrooms*, New York: Harper Collins.

GOODYEAR, R. (1990) *Developing Your Whole school Approach to Assessment Policy*, Slough: NFER Nelson.

GOULD, S. J. (1981) *The Measurement of Man*, Harmondsworth: Penguin.

HALOCHA, J. (1998) *Coordinating geography across the primary school*, London: Falmer Press.

HARLEN, W. (1983) *Guides to Assessment in Education: Science*, London: Macmillan.

HARRIS, A., JAMIESON, I. and RUSS, J. (1996) *School Effectiveness and School Improvement*, London: Pitman Publishing.

HARRISON, M. (1995) 'Developing a Key Stage 2 policy for your subject' in HARRISON, M. (ed) *Developing a Leadership Role in the Key Stage 2 Curriculum*, London: Falmer Press.

HARRISON, M. (1995a) 'Working towards becoming the mathematics coordinator' in HARRISON, M. (ed) *Developing a Leadership Role in the Key Stage 2 Curriculum*, London: Falmer Press.

HARRISON, M. (1995b) 'Getting IT together in Key Stage 2' in HARRISON, M. (ed) *Developing a Leadership Role in the Key Stage 2 Curriculum*, London: Falmer Press.

HARRISON, M. (1998) *Coordinating ICT across the primary school*, London: Falmer Press.

HARRISON, M. and CROSS, A. (1993) 'Developing the skills to become an effective coordinator', in HARRISON, M. (ed) *Beyond the Core Curriculum*, Plymouth: Northcote House.

HARRISON, M. A. and GILL, S. C. (1992) *Primary School Management*, London: Heinemann.

HART, S. (1998) 'A Sorry Tail: Ability, Pedagogy and Educational Reform', *British Journal of Educational Studies*, **46**, 2.

HENNESSY (1998) *Coordinating music across the primary school*, London: Falmer Press.

HMI (1991) *Education in England 1989–90*, London: DES.

HOLLY, P. and SOUTHWORTH, G. (1989) *The Developing School*, London: Falmer Press.

HOPKINS, D., AINSCOW, M. and WEST, M. (1994) *School Improvement in an Era of Change*, London: Cassell.

IMISON, T. (1998) 'Target-setting to raise achievement', *Leading Edge*, London: Institute of Education.

KELLY, V. (1992) 'Introduction' in BLENKIN, G. M. and KELLY, A. V. (eds) *Assessment in Early Childhood Education*, London: PCP.

MATTOCK, G. (1995) 'Religious Education in Key Stage 2' in HARRISON, M. (ed) *Developing a Leadership Role in the Key Stage 2 Curriculum*, London: Falmer Press.

MATTOCK, G. and PRESTON, G. (1995) 'The Religious Education coordinator in the early years' in DAVIES, J. (ed) *Developing a Leadership Role in the Key Stage 1 Curriculum*, London: Falmer Press.

MORRIS, P. (1998) 'Comparative education and educational reform', *Education 3–13*, **26**, 2.

MORTIMER, P., SAMMONS, P., STOLL, L., LEWIS, D. and ECOB, R. (1988) *School matters: The Junior Years*, London, Paul Chapman.

MORTIMER, P., SAMMONS, P., STOLL, L., LEWIS, D. and ECOB, R. (1993) 'Key factors in effective junior schooling' in PREEDY, M. (ed) *Managing the Effective School*, London: PCP.

NAEIAC (1998) 'Teacher assessment in the core subjects at Key Stage 2', *Briefing*, **29**.

NCET (1992) *Assessing IT — Curriculum Support Materials*, Coventry: NCET.

NEWTON, L. and NEWTON, D. (1998) *Coordinating science across the primary school*, London: Falmer Press.

NNP (1998) *National Numeracy Project — Numeracy Lessons*, London: Beam Mathematics.

NOTTINGHAM COUNTY COUNCIL (1994) *Developing Children's Skills in Reviewing Self Assessment Target-setting*, Nottingham County Council: Nottingham.

NOVAK, J.D. and GOWIN, D. B. (1984) *Learning How to Learn*, New York: Cambridge University Press.

OFSTED (1994) *Framework for the Inspection of Schools*, London: HMSO.

OFSTED (1994a) *Assessment Recording and Reporting Report, Her Majesty's Chief Inspector of Schools*, London: HMSO.

OFSTED (1994b) *Primary Matters: A Discussion on Teaching and Learning in Primary Schools*, London: HMSO.

OFSTED (1997) *The Teaching of Number in Three Inner-urban LEAs*, London: HMSO.

OFSTED (1998) *Teacher Assessment in the Core Subjects at Key Stage 2*, London: HMSO.

OFSTED (1998a) *Inspection '98: Supplement to the Inspection Handbooks*, London: HMSO.

OFSTED (1998b) *Inspecting Subjects 3–11: Guidance for Inspectors*, London: HMSO.

PIDGEON, S. (1992) 'Assessment at Key Stage 1: Teacher assessment through record keeping' in BLENKIN, G. M. and KELLY, A. V. (eds) *Assessment in Early Childhood Education*, London: PCP.

PIOTROWSKI, J. (1995) 'Coordinating the art curriculum in Key Stage 2' in HARRISON, M. (ed) *Developing a Leadership Role in the Key Stage 2 Curriculum*, London: Falmer Press.

PLAYFOOT, D., SKELTON, M. and SOUTHWORTH, G. (1989) *The Primary School Management Book*, London: Mary Glasgow Publishers Limited.

PROCTOR, A., ENTWISTLE, M., JUDGE, B., and McKENZIE-MURDOCH, S. (1995) *Learning to Teach in the Primary Classroom*, London: RKP.

QCA (1998) *Maintaining breadth and balance at Key Stages 1 and 2*, London: QCA.

QCA (1998) 'Purpose Organisation Grammar and Style Descriptors'.

RAY, R. (1995) 'Reading at Key Stage 1' in DAVIES, J. (ed) *Developing a Leadership Role in the Key Stage 1 Curriculum*, London: Falmer Press.

RAY, R. (1995a) 'Reading the changes' in HARRISON, M. (ed) *Developing a Leadership Role in the Key Stage 2 Curriculum*, London: Falmer Press.

RAY, R. (1995b) 'Not Sunflowers again! Coordinating art at Key Stage 1' in DAVIES, J. (ed) *Developing a Leadership Role in the Key Stage 1 Curriculum*, London: Falmer Press.

RAYMOND, C. (1998) *Coordinating physical education across the primary school*, London: Falmer Press.

ROBERTS, G. R. (1995) 'Writing' in HARRISON, M. (ed) *Developing a Leadership Role in the Key Stage 2 Curriculum*, London: Falmer Press.

RODGER, R. (1995) 'Geography in the early years: The role of the subject manager' in DAVIES, J. (ed) *Developing a Leadership Role in the Key Stage 1 Curriculum*, London: Falmer Press.

SANDERSON, P. (1995) 'Physical education and dance: leading the way' in HARRISON, M. (ed) *Developing a Leadership Role in the Key Stage 2 Curriculum*, London: Falmer Press.

SCAA (1994) *Key Stage 1 Assessment Folder*, London: HMSO.

SCAA (1994a) *Key Stage 2 Assessment Folder*, London: HMSO.

SCAA (1995) *Planning the Curriculum at Key Stages 1 and 2*, London: HMSO.

SCAA (1995a) *Consistency in Teacher Assessment: Exemplification of Standards, English*, London: SCAA.

SCAA (1995b) *Consistency in Teacher Assessment: Exemplification of Standards, Mathematics*, London: SCAA.

SCAA (1995c) *Consistency in Teacher Assessment: Exemplification of Standards, Science*, London: SCAA.

SCAA (1996) *Key Stage 2 Assessment Arrangements*, London: SCAA.

SCAA (1997a) *Expectations in Information Technology*, London: SCAA.

SCAA (1997b) *Expectations in Geography*, London: SCAA.

SCAA (1997c) *Expectations in Physical Education*, London: SCAA.

SCAA (1997d) *Expectations in History*, London: SCAA.

SCAA (1997e) *Expectations in Art*, London: SCAA.

SCAA (1997f) *Expectations in Design and Technology*, London: SCAA.

SCAA (1997g) *Expectations in Music*, London: SCAA.

SHIPMAN, M. (1993) 'The management of learning: Using the information' in PREEDY, M. (ed) *Managing the Effective School*, London: PCP.

STANDING, A. (1998) 'A curriculum focus', *Managing Schools Today*, June/July 1998.

STEWART, B. and HOCKING, I. (1995) 'Directions in mathematics: The coordinator effect' in DAVIES, J. (ed) *Developing a*

*Leadership Role in the Key Stage 1 Curriculum*, London: Falmer Press.

SUTTON, R. (1991) *Assessment: A Framework for Teaching*, Windsor: NFER-NELSON.

TABBERER, R., HINE, T. and GALLACHER, S. (1996) 'Seven obstacles to effective target setting', *Education Journal*, December pp. 64–65.

TAGG, B. (1996) 'The school in the information age' in TAGG, B. (ed) *Developing a Whole-school IT Policy*, London: Pitman.

TGAT (1988) *National Curriculum Task Group on Assessment and Testing*, Chaired by Professor Paul Black, London: DES.

THOMAS, J. (1998) 'Dealing with problem teachers', *Managing Schools Today*, June/July 1998.

TTA (1998a) *National Standards for Subject Leaders*, London: TTA.

TTA (1998b) *National Standards for Newly Qualified Teachers*, London: TTA.

TTA (1998c) *National Standards for Headteachers*, London: TTA.

TTA (1998d) CD ROM *Assessing your needs*, London: TTA.

TYRRELL, J., WALTERS, M. and MARTIN, T. (1998) *Coordinating English at Key Stage 2*, London: Falmer Press.

WALKER, R. (1995) 'Starting off on the right note' in DAVIES, J. (ed) *Developing a Leadership Role in the Key Stage 1 Curriculum*, London: Falmer Press.

WALKER, T. (1995) 'Sounding the right note' in HARRISON, M. (ed) *Developing a Leadership Role in the Key Stage 2 Curriculum*, London: Falmer Press.

WATERS, M. and MARTIN, T. (1998) *Coordinating English at Key Stage 2*, London: Falmer Press.

WEST, N. (1995) *Middle Management in the Primary School: A Development Guide for Curriculum Leaders, Subject Managers and Senior Staff*, London: David Fulton.

# Index

in-service days (INSET) 40–1, 45,
    50, 54
  effectiveness 56
  planning 77
  target setting 118–25
independent learning 31–2
individual education plans (IEPs)
    23
informal assessment 25, 79,
    80–3
information and communications
    technology (ICT) 32, 74,
    92–3, 98, 137, 153
Information for Parents booklets
    186
inspection week 166–7
inspections 3, 134, 149–68
inspectors 45, 77, 140, 161–2
Internet 158
interpersonal skills 55, 57,
    59–62
intervention 118–22
intervention skill sheet 118
introductions
  assessment policy 170
  marking policy 182
  recording policy 178
involvement 48, 57
  children 28–30
ipsative assessment 143

job descriptions 44, 53, 62
Judge, B. 30

Kelly, V. 11
key issues 84
Key Stages 39, 68–9, 80–1
  agreement trialling 84, 91–4
  ATs 97–8
  end assessments 24
  Mark Schemes 83
  portfolios 138, 139
  statutory obligations 171
  target setting 106–7, 115, 127,
    130

language 51
leadership 44, 61–2
  assessment coordinators 51
  inspections 151–3, 158–9, 166
league tables 3, 4
learning objectives 67, 71
  agreement trialling 84
  class target setting 113
  medium-term planning 3
  target setting 120–1, 123, 126
Letts 81
Level Descriptors 14, 25, 36, 81,
    153
level portfolios 139
Levelled Comprehension Papers
    81
listening 16, 121–2
literacy 13, 84, 105
  inspections 162, 167
  target setting 107
literacy hour 32, 41, 80, 158
local education authorities
    (LEAs) 10, 18, 34–5, 76, 105,
    107, 109, 130
logging sheets 95, 98–9
long-term planning 68–71
low achievers 19

McKenzie-Murdoch, S. 30
management 158–9, 166
Mark Schemes 83–4, 89
marking 27, 43, 45–6, 116–17,
    180–5
Martin, T. 92
mathematics 11–12, 25, 31–2,
    37
  agreement trialling 92
  ATs 97
  consistency 51
  coordinators 48
  inspections 153
  portfolios 133, 137
  subject knowledge 100
  target setting 109
Mattock, G. 93